Book-keeping:
A
Guide for Beginners

Volume 2
FINAL ACCOUNTS

By the same author:

BOOK-KEEPING: A Guide for Beginners
  VOLUME 1 BOOKS TO TRIAL BALANCE

BOOK-KEEPING: A Guide for Beginners
  WORKED SOLUTIONS TO VOLUME 1

BOOK-KEEPING: A Guide for Beginners
  WORKED SOLUTIONS TO VOLUME 2

Also from Stanley Thornes and Hulton:

R. Moody   PRINCIPLES OF ACCOUNTS

Book-keeping:
A
Guide for Beginners

Volume 2
FINAL ACCOUNTS

M. J. Maloney
F.I.C.S., A.C.I.S. (Inter.), Cert. Ed.

Stanley Thornes (Publishers) Ltd

First published in 1988 by:
Stanley Thornes (Publishers) Ltd
Old Station Drive
Leckhampton
CHELTENHAM GL53 0DN
England

British Library Cataloguing in Publication Data

Maloney, M.J.
    Book-keeping: a guide for beginners.
    Vol 2: Final accounts
    1.   Bookkeeping
    I.   Title
    657'.2   HF5635

    ISBN 0-85950-645-2

Typeset by Tech-Set, Gateshead, Tyne & Wear,
in 10/12 Souvenir.
Printed and bound in Great Britain at The Bath Press, Avon.

Contents

Preface

This book is written in the light of years of experience in the business world, followed by twelve years in comprehensive schools teaching accounts to O level and A level. Volume 1 introduces all the basics of book-keeping and follows the steps to be taken by someone beginning in business, up to the first trial balance. It does this through the records of a small firm recently set up by one man. Volume 2 works through this firm's records as far as the final accounts, and then goes on to cover book-keeping for non-profit making organisations, the preparation of final accounts from incomplete records, and the formation of limited companies.

The book will be helpful for students from fourteen years of age who are just beginning to study accounts. Colleges of Further Education which are at present running courses for RSA1, BTEC General, Open Learning, TVEI and CPVE would find all the material is covered in the two volumes. People who are starting their own business, and for whom colleges are running courses, would also benefit from the double-entry book-keeping system.

M.J. Maloney
1987

Introduction

The bookmark that comes with this book shows a trial balance. It is designed so that it can be used for ready reference as the reader works through the early chapters of this volume, and an extract from the trial balance is shown on pp. 56–7. The bookmark will save you time – and patience – as you do not have to turn back to check figures.

This trial balance represents the business position of Mr Tom Robinson, a printer, who has been trading for four months. It also represents the final stage of Volume 1 of this text, *Book-keeping: A Guide for Beginners*, which covers all the aspects of book-keeping involved in the setting up of a business, from the opening of a cash book up to the making of a trial balance.

If the reader is familiar with the basic principles of book-keeping – maintaining the journal, the day books, the ledger, bank reconciliations and so on – then there will be no difficulty in picking up Volume 2 of *Book-keeping: A Guide for Beginners* which will take you up to the preparation of final accounts. However, if anyone is not yet sufficiently familiar with the basics of the subject, then it would be more profitable to read Volume 1 first, before attempting to go on to Volume 2.

Once again, to help maintain interest – and also to make the step-by-step application easier to follow – the book follows the progress of Tom Robinson's business, as far as the final accounts. After that it is necessary to leave Tom for a while in order to deal with more complicated principles, but by the end of Volume 2 we return to his activities to show just how a little knowledge of book-keeping can be very helpful in many different ways. In conclusion there is an outline of what would be the fulfilment of Tom's ambitions – the formation of a limited company.

1

The Trading Account

The trial balance

We have now reached an interesting and important stage. We are about to discover whether Tom Robinson's printing business has made a profit or a loss in the four months that he has been trading. We are about to prepare his **final accounts** for the four months ended December 31, 1985.

(*For convenience, get out the* **trial balance** *sheet on the bookmark. It will be helpful to keep the bookmark out for constant reference while you are working through Chapters 1, 2 and 4.*)

In addition to the figures contained in the trial balance, Tom Robinson would also have a stock of paper, inks, etc., left on his shelves at December 31, 1985, so that he can continue printing at January 1 (at the start of the new financial year). We will assume that this stock (known as **stock in hand**) is valued at £115. This is rarely included in the trial balance but is usually shown as an extra item after the totals, as in the trial balance below.

Extract from Tom's trial balance

Stationery account	S1	22.50	
Travelling expenses	TE1	26.20	
Wages account	W1	400.00	
		£2,394.28	£2,394.28

Stock unsold (or in hand) at December 31, £115·00

From this trial balance we will need to transfer *each* balance into one of the following sections of the final accounts:

- the **trading account**, or
- the **profit and loss account**, or
- the **balance sheet**.

1

The balances used for the trading account are:

- the **stock account** (stock at the start of the business),
- the **purchases**,
- the **purchases returns** (returns outward),
- **wages**,
- **sales**,
- **sales returns** (returns inward).

Closing ledger entries

To transfer the balances above to the trading account it is necessary to 'close' the accounts in Tom's ledger by means of a journal entry.

You will recall from Volume 1 that the journal is the day book which was used to 'open' Tom's cash book and ledger accounts at the start of the business on September 1, 1985. The opening entry from Tom's journal is given below.

Opening entry from Tom's journal

			JOURNAL J/				Folio No.	Assets	Liabilities
Date		Details					Folio No.	Assets	Liabilities
1985 Sept.	1	Cash in hand			dr		CB1	50·00	
		Cash at bank					CB1	600·00	
		Stock	Inks etc.	160·00			SA1	250·00	
			Fluids	90·00					
		Van					V1	450·00	
		Debtor	D. Lewis				L1	120·00	
		Creditors	D. Clarke	160·00			C1		
			W. Long	90·00			L2		
			Avon Motors	450·00			A1		700·00
		Capital	(Balance)				CA1		800·00
								£1500·00	£1500·00
		Being the assets and liabilities of T. Robinson at the start of business September 1, 1985							

Tom's stock account in the ledger at start of business

LEDGER										
DR										**CR**
Date	Details	Folio	£	p	Date	Details	Folio	£	p	
			STOCK	ACC	OUNT	SA1				
1985 Sept. 1	Balance	J1	250	00						

To 'close' the stock account and transfer it to the trading account (the trading account is going to *receive* (dr) £250) we will make the following entry in the journal J2.

Closing entry for Tom's stock account in the journal

Date	Details		Folio No.	Assets	Liabilities
	Trading A/c	dr		£250·00	
	Stock A/c		SA1		£250·00
	Being close of Stock A/c at Dec. 31 1985				

After this entry has been made in the journal and posted to the ledger, the stock account SA1 will be 'closed' and ruled off (see page 5).

Before an account is entered in the ledger it must first have been recorded in a book:
- the purchases day *book*, or
- the sales day *book*, or
- the purchases returns *book*, or
- the sales returns *book*.

Before an account is 'opened' at the start of a business, or 'closed' at the end of a financial period, it must be recorded in the journal, which is a day *book*.

All these *books* are known as the **subsidiary books**.

Tom's balances for the trading account will be entered in the journal before 'closing' the various accounts in his ledger.

Entries in Tom's journal to record balances transferred to the trading account

	JOURNAL J2			
Date	Details	Folio No.	Assets	Liabilities
	Trading account		750·75	
	Stock account	SA1		250·00
	Purchases account	PA1		95·75
	Wages account	W1		400·00
	Sales returns inwards	SR3		5·00
	Being transfer of above balances to close the		£750·75	£750·75
	accounts four months ended December 31, 1985			
	Sales account	SA2	1,150·12	
	Purchases returns outwards	PR1	3·33	
	Trading account			1,153·45
	Being transfer of above balances to close the		£1,153·45	£1,153·45
	accounts four months ended December 31, 1985			

4

The ledger accounts will now be 'closed' and ruled off as follows.

Closing entries in Tom's ledger accounts

LEDGER

DR											CR
Date		Details	Folio	£	p	Date		Details	Folio	£	p
				Stock		Account		SA1			
1985 Sept.	1	Balance	J1	250	00	1985 Dec.	31	Trading account	J2	250	00
				Purchases		Account		PA1			
1985 Dec.	31	Balance	b/d	95	75	1985 Dec.	31	Trading account	J2	95	75
				Purchases		Returns (out)		PR1			
1985 Dec.	31	Trading account	J2	3	33	1985 Dec.	31	Total returns	PRB1	3	33
				Wages		A/c		W1			
1985 Dec.	31	Balance	b/d	400	00	1985 Dec.	31	Trading account	J2	400	00
				Sales		Account		SA2			
1985 Dec.	31	Trading account	J2	1,150	12	1985 Dec.	31	Total sales	SDB1	1,150	12
				Sales		Returns		SR3			
1985 Dec.	31	Total returns	SRB1	5	00	1985 Dec.	31	Trading account	J2	5	00

Stock in hand

A special ledger entry is required for the treatment of **closing stock**, that is stock which is unsold at December 31, 1985. The journal entry on page 3 shows that the stock account for the stock which has been sold since the business started has been 'closed'.

Tom will have counted the individual items of stock and valued them at the **invoice price** (cost) or the **market price**, whichever is *the lower of these two prices*. This will then become the 'opening' stock for his new trading year.

To transfer this figure of £115.00 from the ledger to the trading account requires the journal entry shown below.

Entry in Tom's journal to transfer opening stock for new trading year from the ledger to the trading account

JOURNAL J2

Date	Details		Folio No.	Assets	Liabilities
1985	Stock account	Dr	SA1	115·00	
	Trading account		J2		115·00*
	Being stock unsold at December 31, 1985				

The stock account which we closed above looks like this when the new entry has been made:

Tom's stock account in the ledger showing opening balance for the new trading year

LEDGER

DR									CR	
Date	Details	Folio	£	p	Date	Details	Folio	£	p	
			Stock		Account	SA1				
1985 Sept. 1	Balance	J1	250	00	1985 Dec. 31	Trading account	J2	250	00	
1986 Jan. 1	Balance	J2	115	00						

*In practice, it is usual to *debit* this figure in the trading account (see page 7).

The trading account

Using ledger paper we will start Tom's trading account from the balance shown on the bookmark.

Extract from Tom's trading account

LEDGER										
DR										**CR**
Date	Details	Folio	£	p	Date	Details	Folio	£	p
			TRADING	ACCOUNT					
	Four months ended December 31,1985								
	Stock at Sept.1,1985		250	00		Sales		1150	12
	Purchases £95·75				Less	Returns(in)		5	00
Less	Returns(out) 3·33		92	42				1145	12
			342	42					
	Wages		400	00					
			742	42					
Less Stock unsold at 31·12·1985			115	00					
	Cost of goods sold		627	42					

Explanation of the entries

1) *The debit column*
   Stock at the *beginning* of the period   250.00
   Purchases are shown *minus* returns   92.42
               Total   342.42

   Add Wages   400.00
           742.42

   Less Stock unsold at the end of the period   115.00

   Cost of goods sold   £627.42

- *Wages*. In the above trading account wages are shown as £400.

  Wages *always* represent money paid *weekly* to workers who produce the goods or handle the stock. In Tom's case this would be his assistant. In the case of a large business, e.g. a supermarket, it would be the shop assistants, warehouse staff or anyone who handles the stock.

  Because wages are part of the cost of making the goods ready for sale wages are *always* shown as an expense in the trading account.

- *Stock unsold*. A figure of £115 has been deducted at the end of the trading account because this stock has not yet been sold. In fact it will be shown at the start of the next trading account as the opening stock for the new trading period, i.e. January 1, 1986.

- *Cost of goods sold*. The figure to which a percentage is added to arrive at the selling price.

2) *The credit column*
   It is easy to remember the details for this side – there are only two:

   - *Sales* (£1,150.12). This is the total value of the goods sold and includes a percentage of profit.
   - *Sales returns* (£5.00). These are deducted because the goods have been returned and are back on the shelves to be sold again.

Having explained each of the entries we are now ready to balance the trading account by totalling the credit side (sales), which gives £1,145.12, and deducting the total of the debit side (expenses), £627.42. This gives us a balance of £517.70 which we call the **gross profit**. It is explained in more detail below.

Gross profit

> The gross profit is the difference between the selling price of the goods and the cost of sales.

The definition of gross profit is important and should be memorised.

Here is a simple example:

> I buy a book for £3 and pay postage expenses of 17p. The total cost is therefore £3.17.

> I sell the book for £4.00. I have made a gross profit of 83p.

The trading account for this simple transaction would be:

8

Simple trading account showing gross profit

LEDGER											
DR											**CR**
Date		Details	Folio	£	p	Date		Details	Folio	£	p
				TRADING		ACCOUNT					
		Purchases		3	00			Sales		4	00
		Postage (or carriage)		0	17						
		Gross profit		0	83						
				£ 4	00					£ 4	00

We will now complete Tom's trading account and rule it off in the same way as a ledger account.

Completion of Tom's trading account

LEDGER											
DR											**CR**
Date		Details	Folio	£	p	Date		Details	Folio	£	p
				TRADING		ACCOUNT					
		Four months ended December 31, 1985									
		Stock at Sept. 1, 1985		250	00			Sales		1,150	12
		Purchases £95.75					Less	Returns (in)		5	00
Less		Returns (out) 3.33		92	42					1,145	12
				342	42						
		Wages		400	00						
				742	42						
Less	Stock unsold at 31·12·1985			115	00						
		Cost of goods sold		627	42						
		Balance being gross		517	70						
		profit S/a to Profit and										
		Loss A/c									
				£ 1,145	12					£ 1,145	12

It is important to mention here further items which, although not necessary for Tom's trading account, could be included in examination questions.

1) *Gross loss*

It is possible for a **gross loss** to arise in the trading account. If the cost of selling the goods exceeds the *net* sales, resulting in a loss, the gross loss will be shown on the *credit* side of the trading account as shown below:

Trading account showing gross loss

LEDGER											
DR											**CR**
Date		Details	Folio	£	p	Date		Details	Folio	£	p
				TRADING	ACCOUNT						
				Period ended				......,19....			
		Stock at start		250	00			Sales		600	00
		Purchases £95·75					Less	Returns(in)		5	00
Less		Returns(out) 3·33		92	42					595	00
				342	42			Balance being gross			
		Wages		400	00			loss c/d to Profit and			
				742	42			Loss A/c		32	42
Less stock unsold at .....,19..				115	00						
		Cost of goods sold		£627	42					£627	42

2) There are two other relevant expenses which may be included in examination questions:
   - *Carriage in*. This is a charge made by the carrier, by road, rail or by the post office, for delivering goods purchased by the firm.
   - *Freight*. This is the charge made for goods carried by ship or air.

If either or both of these expenses occur in a trial balance they would be shown below the wages entry as part of the costs.

Trading account showing carriage in

LEDGER										
DR									**CR**	
Date	Details	Folio	£	p	Date	Details	Folio	£	p
			TRADING	ACCOUNT						
			Period ended				,19			
	Stock at ....,19..		250	00		Sales		1,150	12
	Purchases £95·75				Less	Returns (in)		5	00
Less	Returns (out) 3·33		92	42				1,145	12
			342	42					
	Wages £400·00								
	Carriage in £70·00								
	Freight £80·00		550	00					
			892	42					
Less	Stock in hand at ....,19..		115	00					
	Cost of goods sold		777	42					
	Balance being gross		367	70					
	profit c/d to Profit								
	and Loss A/c								
			£1,145	12				£1,145	12

3) Goods may be taken from stock at cost price for the owner's private use.

If Tom used some of his paper stocks to have some printing done for his private use and did not pay for it, this would be treated as **drawings in kind**.

For example, let us say Tom took paper valued £30. It would reduce the purchases account by £30 (a credit) and be debited to his drawings account.

This would need a journal entry as follows.

Journal entry to record drawings in kind

JOURNAL J2					
Date	Details		Folio No.	Assets	Liabilities
	Drawings account	dr		30·00	
	Purchases account				30·00
	Being stock used for private work of				
	Mr. Robinson on . . . . , 19. . .				

Chapter 1 Exercises

The trading account

1 *From the following extracts from Jane Blackmore's trial balance prepare a trading account for the year ended December 31, 1985:*

Stock at start	£3,000
Purchases	£13,260
Stock taken for Jane's personal use (drawings in kind)	£122
Returns outward	£200
Wages	£2,200
Stock in hand at December 31	£2,450
Sales	£18,000
Returns inward	£422

2 *Prepare Sandy Small's trading account from the following balances for three months ended May 31, 1986:*

Stock at start	£4,300
Purchases	£28,000
Wages	£7,900
Carriage in	£185
Stock at May 31	£3,800
Sales	£49,900

3 *Prepare K. Patel's trading account from the following extracts from the trial balance for the year ended December 31, 1985:*

Stock at start	£2,500
Purchases	£57,200
Goods taken for personal use	£160
Returns outward	£180
Wages	£1,600
Freight charges	£250
Stock at December 31, 1985	£3,675
Sales	£72,340

4 *Prepare J. Gregson's trading account from the following details for the month ended December 31, 1985:*

Stock at start	£2,800
Purchases	£24,000
Wages	£4,580
Sales	£35,000
Returns inward	£500
Stock in hand at December 31, 1985	£4,000

Closing journal entries and transfer of ledger balances to the trading account

1 **a)** *Show the 'closing' journal entries for the following accounts, and*
b) *close the ledger accounts for the year ended December 31, 1985, in the books of Le Petit Children's Wear.*

Stock account (SA1)	£2,450
Purchases account (PA1)	£14,620
Wages (W1)	£1,400
Purchases returns (PR1)	£225
Sales (S1)	£18,000
Stock in hand at December 31, 1985	£1,000

Answers are given in the *Worked Solutions.*

2   The Profit and Loss Account

Having completed the trading account we have arrived at Tom Robinson's gross profit for the quarter. On page 9 we see that this was £517.70.

But Tom needs to know his actual profit (**net profit**), and so he has to deduct from the gross profit all the other expenses which did not figure in the trading account.

These expenses are shown in the debit column of the trial balance, which is on the bookmark. They are:

- Bank charges
- Discount allowed
- Electricity
- Petrol
- Postage
- Rent
- Rates
- Stationery
- Travelling

To find Tom's net profit we must now produce a profit and loss account.

First, all the accounts for the above expenses must be closed in the ledger by means of a journal entry.

Tom's journal entry to close expense accounts

JOURNAL J3						
Date		Details	Folio No.	Assets	Liabilities
1985 Dec.	31	Profit + loss a/c		315.95	
✓	✓	Bank charges	BC1		48.00
✓	✓	Discount allowed	DA2		2.25
✓	✓	Electricity	E1		110.00
✓	✓	Petrol	P1		12.00
✓	✓	Postage	P3		5.00
✓	✓	Rent account	R1		60.00
✓	✓	Rates	R2		30.00
✓	✓	Stationery	S1		22.50
✓	✓	Travelling	TE1		26.20
				£315.95	£315.95
		Being transfer of balances to profit + loss account four months ended December 31, 1985			

The 'closed' ledger accounts will look as follows. Note that the entries in the debit column are taken from the accounts balanced on page 93 of Volume 1.

Closing entries for the expense accounts in Tom's ledger

LEDGER									
DR									**CR**
Date	Details	Folio	£	p	Date	Details	Folio	£	p

BANK CHARGES ACCOUNT BC1

Date	Details	Folio	£	p	Date	Details	Folio	£	p
1986 Jan. 1	Balance	b/d	48	00	1985 Dec. 31	Profit + loss a/c	J3	48	00

DISCOUNT ALLOWED ACCOUNT DA2

Date	Details	Folio	£	p	Date	Details	Folio	£	p
1986 Jan. 1	Balance	b/d	2	25	1985 Dec. 31	Profit + loss a/c	J3	2	25

ELECTRICITY E1

Date	Details	Folio	£	p	Date	Details	Folio	£	p
1985 Nov. 3	Bank	CB3	110	00	1985 Dec. 31	Profit + loss a/c	J3	110	00

PETROL P1

Date	Details	Folio	£	p	Date	Details	Folio	£	p
1985 Dec. 5	Petty cash	PC1	12	00	1985 Dec. 31	Profit + loss a/c	J3	12	00

POSTAGE P3

Date	Details	Folio	£	p	Date	Details	Folio	£	p
1985 Dec. 5	Petty cash	PC1	5	00	1985 Dec. 31	Profit + loss a/c	J3	5	00

RENT ACCOUNT R1

Date	Details	Folio	£	p	Date	Details	Folio	£	p
1986 Jan. 1	Balance	b/d	60	00	1985 Dec. 31	Profit + loss a/c	J3	60	00

RATES ACCOUNT R2

Date	Details	Folio	£	p	Date	Details	Folio	£	p
1986 Jan. 1	Balance	b/d	30	00	1985 Dec. 31	Profit + loss a/c	J3	30	00

STATIONERY S1

Date	Details	Folio	£	p	Date	Details	Folio	£	p
1986 Jan. 1	Balance	b/d	22	50	1985 Dec. 31	Profit + loss a/c	J3	22	50

TRAVELLING EXPENSES TE1

Date	Details	Folio	£	p	Date	Details	Folio	£	p
1985 Dec. 5	Petty cash	PC1	26	20	1985 Dec. 31	Profit + loss a/c	J3	26	20

Tom's profit and loss account showing expenses

PROFIT AND LOSS ACCOUNT						
DR Four months ended December 31, 1985						**CR**
Details	£	p	Details		£	p
Expenses (or losses)						
Bank charges	48	00				
Discount allowed	2	25				
Electricity	110	00				
Petrol	12	00				
Postage	5	00				
Rent	60	00				
Rates	30	00				
Stationery	22	50				
Travelling expenses	26	20				

These are all the 'losses'. We will now transfer the gains. There is only one in the trial balance, i.e., the discount received of £11.70, but the trading account shows Tom made a gross profit of £517.70.

We must now transfer both of these items into the profit and loss account as 'gains' on the credit side.

First the gross profit will be shown as a gain in the profit and loss account:

18

Tom's profit and loss account including gross profit

PROFIT AND LOSS ACCOUNT

DR	Four months ended December 31, 1985					CR
Details	£	p	Details	£	p
Bank charges	48	00	Gross profit b/d from the		
Discount allowed	2	25	trading account.	517	70
Electricity	110	00	Discount received	11	70
Petrol	12	00			
Postage	5	00			
Rent	60	00			
Rates	30	00			
Stationery	22	50			
Travelling expenses	26	20			
Total losses	£315	95	Total gains	£529	40

Tom's total 'gains' are	529.40	
minus total losses	315.95	
the difference of	£213.45	being his net (real) profit.

> Net profit is the gross profit *plus* other credits *minus* overhead expenses.

In the profit and loss account shown above a line has been drawn under expenses and the total entered underneath. *In practice* this should be done in pencil *only* to help you subtract the debits from the credits. The pencil figures can then be erased in order to produce the finished account in good style as shown on page 20.

The discount received account would also be closed in the ledger by making an appropriate entry in the Journal.

Closing entry for the discount received account in Tom's journal

		JOURNAL J3				
Date		Details	Folio No.	Assets	Liabilities	
		Discount received A/c	DR3	11·70		
		Profit and loss A/c			11·70	
		Being close of discount received account				
		four months ended December 31, 1985				

Tom's completed profit and loss account

	PROFIT AND LOSS ACCOUNT					
DR	Four months ended December 31, 1985					**CR**
Details		£	p	Details	£	p
Bank charges		48	00	Gross profit b/d from		
Discount allowed		2	25	trading account	517	70
Electricity		110	00	Discount received	11	70
Petrol		12	00			
Postage		5	00			
Rent		60	00			
Rates		30	00			
Stationery		22	50			
Travelling expenses		26	20			
Balance being net profit c/d to the balance sheet		213	45			
		£529	40		£529	40

The profit and loss account which we have just completed is comparatively simple because after only four months Tom's business is still quite small. But Tom expects that by the time his final accounts are prepared, which will be at the end of one year's complete trading, his business will have expanded. Therefore, we can expect that his profit and loss account will have to contain many more entries as the number of expenses will also have increased.

1) The obvious expenses in the day-to-day running of any business: heating, lighting, various repairs, telephone, stationery, cleaning, etc.

2) The question of Value Added Tax (VAT) will have to be considered. The subject is dealt with in Chapter 3, for entries in the subsidiary books. Entries in the final accounts are shown in Chapters 9, 14 and 16.

3) Bank charges, loans and overdrafts may also have to be considered (see Volume 1, Chapter 4).

4) **Bad debts** are losses which Tom is almost bound to have to face. They arise when goods sold on credit have not been paid for, and the accounts are long overdue. (Chapter 5 will go into this aspect in more detail.)

5) **Salaries** may also need to be considered. If Tom's business were to increase sufficiently he might well employ office and sales staff. These employees would be paid a salary. A salary is a monthly payment and (unlike wages) it does not appear in the trading account but must *always* be included in the profit and loss account.

    If the salesman brings in a lot of business, Tom might also pay him **commission**, i.e. a percentage of his total sales. This would also have to be shown as an expense in the profit and loss account.

6) **Carriage outward** or **distribution expenses** are charges made for goods being transported by road, rail or post, from a firm to a customer. If the goods are carried by sea or air the charges are known as **freight charges**.

- Carriage in is the charge for the goods *to the firm* and is always shown as an *expense* in the trading account (goods are carried *in* to the business).
- Carriage out is the charge for goods being sent *out* to a customer and is therefore shown in the profit and loss account as an *expense*.

It is important to bear in mind that there could be a difference between a 'theoretical' question in an examination paper and actual business practice.

In an examination paper the question may instruct you to prepare the trading account and a profit and loss account from a given trial balance. In this case these balances must be entered directly into the trading account and profit and loss account without any reference to the journal.

However, in a business, *all* transfers from, or into, the ledger *must* be made by use of the journal. This ensures that there is a complete record of all business transactions.

Chapter 2 Exercises

The profit & loss account

1 *Prepare a profit and loss account from the following balances taken from the trial balance of W. Wentworth, year ended June 30, 1986:*

Gross profit for the year	£13,660
Expenses	
Salaries	£4,780
Cleaning	£410
Repairs to office machines	£630
Rent	£720
Heating and lighting	£400
Telephone	£180
Travelling expenses	£350
Discount received	£40

2 *Prepare a profit and loss account from the following balances taken from the trial balance of M. Sharif, year ended August 30, 1985:*

Gross profit for the year	£12,500
Rent and rates	£2,500
Discount allowed	£350
Discount received	£180
Salaries	£2,480
Electricity	£450
Office expenses	£2,400
Bank charges	£150
Stationery and advertising	£450

3 *From the following balances prepare N. Jarmala's profit and loss account for the month ended June 30, 1986:*

Gross profit from the trading account	£8,350
Discount allowed	£260
Petrol	£150
Rent	£300
Rates	£510
Electricity	£350
Rent received	£206
Salaries	£800
Discount received	£85

4 a) *Show the journal entries for the following balances in order to transfer them from the ledger to the profit and loss account at December 31, 1985:*

Bank charges (BC1)	£90
Stationery a/c (S2)	£220
Travelling expenses (T4)	£200
Electricity a/c (E1)	£350

b) *Close the ledger accounts for each of the above.*
Insert folio numbers for each entry.

Answers are given in the *Worked Solutions.*

3

Value Added Tax

One very important item for a business is **Value Added Tax** (VAT). This is a tax levied by HM Customs and Excise on the goods and services purchased and sold by a person or company that is registered for VAT. Registration is compulsory if turnover is over a certain amount,* but a person or company with a lower turnover can register. Some goods are exempt from VAT, others are either charged at the current standard rate or are zero rated.* Details of all aspects of VAT are obtainable from HM Customs and Excise, together with registration forms and other information.

The VAT registered person must keep account of all VAT paid on purchases (**input VAT**) and all VAT collected from sales (**output VAT**). If the outputs are more than the inputs (and they generally are) the balance is paid to HM Customs and Excise every three months.

To illustrate how VAT should be recorded we will follow the business of J.R. Hyland who runs a joinery and property repair business as well as a retail hardware store. The invoices for the following transactions for August and September are to be entered in the books of J.R. Hyland.

Aug. 15   Bought on credit from Greendyke Tools, power tools for resale, £212.97 plus 15% VAT.

Aug. 25   Bought on credit from Crown Embassy, 1 patio door £162.69, less $2\frac{1}{2}$% trade discount, plus 15% VAT – Invoice No. 2631.

Sept. 1   Supplied and fitted a patio door £247.28 including VAT, Job No. 76—L. Coyne.

Sept. 12   Supplied and fitted doors £223.96 including VAT, Job No. 77—E. Mancini.

Sept. 15   Paid Greendyke Tools £244.91 by cheque.

Sept. 28   Till receipts for the month £2,463.30 including £321.30 VAT.

Sept. 28   Received a cheque from E. Mancini £223.96.

Sept. 28   Transferred £2,000 cash into bank account.

Purchases and VAT

First, we will consider the purchases from suppliers to J.R. Hyland. The following pages show the invoices received followed by the entries to be made in the purchases day book, the cash book and the ledger.

*Subject to alteration in the annual Budget.

Sales invoice from Greendyke Tools to J.R. Hyland Joinery and Hardware Stores

Sales Invoice No. **A 10995**

Greendyke Tools

Greendyke Limited,
Worthing Lane
Manchester M32 T5

Telephone: 061 8218001
VAT Reg. No: 223-3269-92

J.R. Hyland
Joinery & Hardware Stores
6 Treelane Avenue
Old Felton
GATESHEAD, Tyne & Wear
NE8 3L

Date/Tax Point 15/8/85

Goods by: Road ✔
Rail
Post

Your order: **A36** 10/8/85

Quantity	Description Price	Amount excluding VAT	VAT Rate	VAT Net
1	Power Plane 330 watt motor	42.99		
1	Power Drill-Parts model 707	104.99		
1	Circular Saw 7¼"	64.99		
			15%	31.94
Terms: **Net**		212.97		31.94
	VAT	31.94		
	Total	244.91		

*PDB1/1**

*This is the invoice number shown in the purchases day book.

Sales invoice from Crown Embassy to J.R. Hyland Joinery and Hardware Stores

Crown Embassy

Joinery and Timber
Suppliers to the
Trade only.

Sales Invoice No. 2631

Hardwood Works · Farnwork Street
Dunston · Tyne and Wear · NE9 6L

Telephone
VAT Reg No. 053 · 2901 · 24

J.R. Hyland
Joinery & Hardware Stores
6 Treelane Avenue
Old Felton
GATESHEAD Tyne & Wear NE8 3L

your order 422 24/8/85
tax point/date 25th August 1985

goods despatched by

road   rail   post   collect
                        ✓

Ref No	Description	Quantity	Price per unit	Cost
2210	Patio Door Double glazed-sliding	1	£162.69	£162.69
Less	Trade Discount 2½%			4.06
				£158.63
		VAT @	15%	23.80
			Total	£182.43

Terms: **Net**

PD81/2*

*This is the invoice number shown in the purchases day book. The invoices are filed in numerical order with the most recent on top in the file.

The invoices are entered in the purchases day book as follows:

Entry of invoices in the purchases day book

PURCHASES DAY BOOK PDB1

Date		Details		Invoice No.	Folio	Net	Input VAT	Total
1985								
Aug	15	Greendyke Tools						
		Goods		1/1	G1	212.97	31.94	244.91
✓	25	Crown Embassy						
		Goods	162.69	1/2				
		Less Trade Discount	4.06		CE1	158.63	23.80	182.43
Sept	30	Totals for the month				371.60	55.74	
						(PAI)	(VI)	

The payments are entered in the cash book as follows:

Entry of payments in the cash book

CASH BOOK (Payments side)   CR

Date		Details	Folio	Discount	Input VAT	Net	Cash	Bank
Sept.	15	Greendyke Tools	G1					244.91
✓	28	Bank	(C)				2,000.00	
✓	30	Balance	c/d				463.30	1,979.05
							2,463.30	2,223.96

Note:
- The *separate* entries for VAT are recorded in the personal accounts in the ledger (credit side).
- The *total* amount paid is recorded in the VAT account (debit side). This is the total of the Input VAT column in the purchases day book.

The purchases day book and cash book entries are then posted to the ledger:

Posting of entries in the purchases day book and cash book in the ledger

				LEDGER				
DR								**CR**
Date	Details	Folio	£ p	Date	Details	Folio	£ p
				Greendyke Tools G1				
1985				1985			
Sept. 15	Bank	CB1	244.91	Aug. 15	Purchases	PDB1	212.97
				15	VAT	PDB1	31.94
			244.91				244.91
				Crown Embassy CE1				
1985				1985			
Sept. 30	Balance	c/d	182.43	Aug. 25	Purchases	PDB1	158.63
				25	VAT	PDB1	23.80
			182.43				182.43
				Oct. 1	Balance	b/d	182.43
				Purchases A/C PA1				
1985							
Sept. 30	Total for Aug. & Sept.	PDB1	371.60				
				VAT V1				
1985	(input)						
Sept. 30	Total purchases	PDB1	£55.74				

The above ledger entries are shown in the traditional "T" style, so called because the horizontal rule at the top and the double vertical rules in the middle divide the page up to form the letter T, thereby separating the debit side from the credit side. This type of ruling has been in use for many years in double-entry book-keeping.

The modern style of ledger entries is known as the **running balance method** and is read from left to right across the entire page. It is said to be easier to read at a glance and bank statements generally use this form for presenting accounts (see Volume 1, page 18). As a result of the increasing use of computers in business, the running balance method has become more widely used for ledger entries throughout book-keeping.

For examination purposes both the traditional "T" style and the running balance method are equally acceptable. The ledger entries shown on page 28 for J.R. Hyland would look as follows using the modern running balance method.

Posting of ledger entries using the running balance method

PURCHASE LEDGER					
Date	Details	Folio	Debit	Credit	Balance
	Greendyke Tools G1				
1985					
Aug. 15	Purchases	PDB1		212.97	212.97
✓ 15	VAT	PDB1		31.94	244.91
Sept. 15	Bank	CB1	244.91		— —
	Crown Embassy CE1				
1985					
Aug. 25	Purchases	PDB1		158.63	158.63
✓ 25	VAT	PDB1		23.80	182.43
	Purchases A/C PA1	PDB1			
1985					
Sept. 30	Total for August and September		371.60		371.60
	VAT (input) A/C V1				
1985					
Sept. 30	Total purchases	PDB1	55.74		55.74

Cash purchases with VAT

Let us assume that J.R. Hyland purchases sundry hardware items on October 1, 1985 and pays cash to the value of £87.50 which includes input VAT at 15%. The cash book entry will be:

Entry of cash purchases in the cash book

	CASH BOOK CB1 (Payments side)						CR
Date	Details	Folio	Discount	Input VAT	Net	Cash	Bank
1985		V1					
Oct. 1	Purchases	PA1	—	11.42	76.08	87.50	—

The purchases and VAT accounts will be:

Posting cash purchases in the ledger

			LEDGER				
DR							**CR**
Date	Details	Folio	£ p	Date	Details	Folio	£ p
			Purchases Account PA1				
1985							
Oct. 1	Cash	CB1	76.08				
			VAT Account V1				
1985							
Oct. 1	Purchases	CB1	11.42				

Sales and VAT

Let us now consider invoices relating to sales from J.R. Hyland's shop, and work done by him.

Sales invoice from J.R. Hyland for work carried out

J R Hyland

Invoice/Job No 76

JOINERY & HARDWARE STORES

6 Treelane Avenue, Old Felton, Gateshead, Tyne and Wear, NE8 3L.   Telephone 091 361200

VAT Reg No 23–9620–80
Date: 1/9/85

Mrs. L. Coyne
The Larches, 2 Limekiln Lane
GATESHEAD, Tyne & Wear NE8 4B

Quantity	Description	Price	Amount	VAT Rate	VAT Net
1	To supplying & fitting: 6ft Patio door – Dining Room		215.03	15%	32.25
			215.03		32.25
		VAT	32.25		
		Total	247.28		

SDB1/1

Sales invoice from J.R. Hyland for work carried out

J R Hyland

Invoice/Job No 77

JOINERY & HARDWARE STORES

6 Treelane Avenue, Old Felton, Gateshead, Tyne and Wear, NE8 3L.   Telephone 091 361200

VAT Reg No 23–9620–80
Date: 12/9/85

Mrs. E. Mancini
'Shangrila', Maryport Road
DUNSTON, Tyne & Wear NE9 4A

Quantity	Description	Price	Amount	VAT Rate	VAT Net
1	To supplying & fitting: Hardwood door 6' 10" × 2' 10"		68.90		
1	Up and over garage door 7' × 7' 6"		76.95		
			145.85	15%	21.87
	Labour		48.90	15%	7.34
			194.75		29.21
		VAT	29.21		
		Total	£223.96		

SDB1/2

32

The invoices are entered in the sales day book as follows:

Entry of invoices in the sales day book

SALES DAY BOOK SDB1							
Date		Details	Invoice No.	Folio	Net	Output VAT	Total
1985							
Sept.	1	L. Coyne Job No. 76	SDB1	C1	215.03	32.25	247.28
✓	12	E. Mancini Job No. 77	SDB2	M1	194.75	29.21	223.96
Sept.	30	Totals for the month			409.78	61.46	471.24
					(SA1)	(V1)	

Mr Hyland also transferred £2,000 cash from his till into his firm's bank account.

Bank paying-in slip

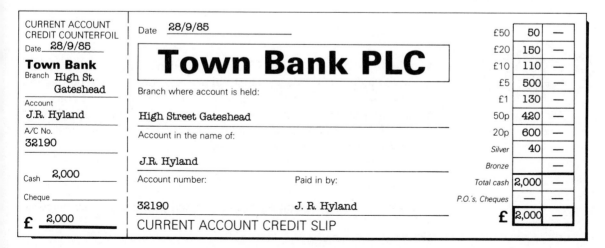

The receipts are entered in the cash book as follows:

Entry of receipts and £2,000 cash transferred to the bank in the cash book

CASH BOOK (Receipts side)

Date		Details	Folio	Discount Allowed	Output VAT	Net	Cash	Bank
1985			V1					
Sept.	28	Till receipts	SA1		321.30	2,142.00	2,463.00	
✔	28	Cash	(C)					2,000.00
✔	29	E. Mancini	M1					223.96
					321.30	2,142.00	2,463.30	2,223.96
Oct.	1	Balance*	B/d				463.30	1,979.05

Note:
- The separate entries for VAT are recorded in the personal accounts in the ledger (debit side). The total amount received is recorded in the VAT account (credit side) taken from the sales day book.
- Because there are cash sales, i.e. till receipts, the VAT is recorded in the VAT account and there are *two* folio numbers in the folio column in the cash book as shown above.

The sales day book and cash book entries are posted to the ledger as follows:

*The cash book was balanced on September 30 (see page 27).

34

Posting of entries in the sales day book and cash book in the ledger

LEDGER							
DR							**CR**
Date	Details	Folio	£ p	Date	Details	Folio	£ p

L. Coyne C1

Date	Details	Folio	£ p	Date	Details	Folio	£ p
1985				1985			
Sept. 1	Job No. 76	SDB1	215.03	Sept. 30	Balance	c/d	247.28
✓ 1	VAT	SDB1	32.25				
			247.28				247.28
Oct. 1	Balance	b/d	247.28				

E. Mancini M1

Date	Details	Folio	£ p	Date	Details	Folio	£ p
1985				1985			
Sept. 12	Job No. 77	SDB1	194.75	Sept. 29	Bank	CB1	223.96
✓ 12	VAT	SDB1	29.21				
			223.96				223.96

Sales A/C SA1

Date	Details	Folio	£ p	Date	Details	Folio	£ p
1985				1985			
Oct. 1	Balance	c/d	2,551.78	Sept. 30	Total for month	SDB1	409.78
				30	Till receipts	CB1	2,142.00
			2,551.78				2,551.78
				Oct. 1	Balance	b/d	2,551.78

VAT V1 (Output)

Date	Details	Folio	£ p	Date	Details	Folio	£ p
				1985			
				Sept. 30	Till	CB1	321.30
				30	Sales	SDB1	61.46

The entries on page 35 recorded in the traditional style can also be written using the more modern running balance method:

Posting of ledger entries using the running balance method

SALES LEDGER

Date	Details	Folio	Debit	Credit	Balance
L. Coyne C1					
1985					
Sept. 1	Job No. 76	SDB1	215.03		215.03
✓ 1	VAT	SDB1	32.25		247.28
E. Mancini M1					
1985					
Sept. 12	Job No. 77	SDB1	194.75		194.75
✓ 12	VAT	SDB1	29.21		223.96
✓ 29	Bank	CB1		223.96	— —
Sales A/C SA1					
1985					
Sept. 30	Total for month	SDB1		409.78	409.78
✓ 30	Till receipts	CB1		2,142.00	2,551.78
VAT (output) A/C V1					
1985					
Sept. 30	Till	CB1		321.30	321.30
✓ 30	Sales	SDB1		61.46	382.76

Checking the figures

In order to satisfy himself that his VAT figures are correct Mr Hyland takes out a trial balance. Since the trial balance agrees, Mr Hyland is able to make the correct return to HM Customs and Excise. A simplified VAT Return Form for use by HM Customs and Excise VAT office is given after the trial balance.

Trial balance to check VAT figures

TRIAL BALANCE
August – September 1985

Date	Details	Folio	Assets	Liabilities
	Cash in hand		463.30	
	Bank		1,979.05	
	Crown Embassy			182.43
	Coyne, L.		247.28	
	Sales			2,551.78
	Purchases		371.60	
	VAT (input)		55.74	
	VAT (output)			
	Sales	(SDB1)		61.46
	Till	(CB1)		321.30
			£3,116.97	£3,116.97

Simplified VAT return form

VAT ACCOUNT

INPUT		OUTPUT	
1985	£ p	1985	£ p
August		August	
		Sales	
Purchases (PDB1) (credit)	55.74	September	
		Credit sales (SDB1)	61.46
	£55.74	Cash sales (CB1)	321.30
		Total output	382.76
		Less Total input	55.74
		Balance due to HM Customs	£327.02

The treatment of VAT is further complicated when we consider goods that have been returned (inwards and outwards), discounts have been allowed and received, and when carriage in and out is involved. The following sections show how these matters are dealt with in relation to VAT.

Returns inward and VAT

It sometimes happens in the course of business that a customer will return goods to the seller. Perhaps the goods are not up to the required standard, or have been damaged in transit, or there is some other valid reason why they cannot be accepted for sale. A **credit note** will often be issued to the value of the returned goods.

Credit notes are recorded in a book known as the **returns inward book**, so called because the goods are returned *in* to the firm. The rulings are the same as those of the sales day book with the VAT column headed "Output VAT".

To illustrate the method or recording returns inwards in connection with VAT, we will take the following example from J.R. Hyland's hardware shop.

On October 2, 1985 a customer, Mrs P. Tiptree, purchased a set of 5 non-stick heavy gauge pans valued at £69.75. She had them charged to her Budget Account.

On October 7 she returned the chip pan, valued at £22.99, because the lid was out of alignment. As there was not a replacement in stock she asked for her account to be credited with £22.99 (this included 15% output VAT).

To record this:

- an entry would be made in the returns inward book;
- Mrs Tiptree's account would be credited;
- the VAT account in the ledger would also be debited.

Entry of goods returned in the returns inward book

RETURNS INWARD BOOK				RIB1			
Date	Details	Credit No.	Folio	Item	Net	Output VAT	Total
Oct. 7	Tiptree, P.	12	BT30	1 non-stick frying pan	19.99	3.00 ⓥ⒤	22.99
	Faulty lid out of alignment. Credited customer's account		7/10/85				

Entry of goods returned in customer's account

ACCOUNT NO. BT30 Mrs P. Tiptree 16 Sandstone Road DUNSTON					
Date	Details	Folio	Debit	Credit	Balance
1985					
Oct. 2	Pans set of 5	SDB1	60.65		60.65
✓ 2	VAT	SDB1	9.10		69.75
✓ 7	Returns in	RIB1		19.99	49.76
✓ 7	VAT	RIB1		3.00	46.76

Adjustment of VAT account in the ledger

LEDGER								
DR								**CR**
Date	Details	Folio	£ p	Date	Details	Folio	£ p	
			VAT A/C V1					
1985								
Oct. 7	P. Tiptree	RIB1	3.00					
	Credit note							

Returns outward and VAT

We have seen that credit notes are issued for goods sent back in to the seller for various reasons. So too credit notes are issued for goods purchased and returned *out* to the supplier for valid reasons. These credit notes will be recorded in a book called the **returns outward book**. It is ruled in the same way as the purchases day book with a column for the input VAT.

The VAT regulations, however, require the following information to be shown on credit notes for returns outwards:

- the identifying number and date of issue;
- the name and address of the firm issuing the credit note;
- the customer's name and address;
- the reason for the credit;
- the description which identifies the goods or services;
- the quantity and amount credited for each description;
- the total amount credited, excluding VAT;
- the rate and amount of VAT credited.

(Extracted from HM Customs and Excise Notice No. 700, page 37.)

To illustrate how this is dealt with let us return to J.R. Hyland's business. On September 28 Mr Hyland returned to Greendyke Tools an orbital sanding machine which had cost £16.25 plus 15% VAT of £2.43 because the mechanism was found to be faulty.

The steps to be taken are as follows:

1) J.R. Hyland must record the returned goods in the returns *outward* book.
2) The goods must be returned to Greendyke Tools who will enter it in their returns *inward* book.
3) Greendyke Tools will issue a credit note.
4) J.R. Hyland will record the credit note in his ledger.

Entry of returned goods in returns outward book

RETURNS OUTWARD BOOK ROB1								
Date		Details	Credit No.	Folio	Item	Net	Input VAT	Total
1985								
Sept.	28	Greendyke Tools	C223	G1	1 Orbital sanding machine	16.25	2.43	18.68
		Reason: faulty mechanism.						

Entry of returned goods in supplier's returns inward book

RETURNS INWARD BOOK RIB1								
Date		Details	Credit No.	Folio	Item	Net	Output VAT	Total
1985								
Oct.	1	J.R. Hyland	C223	JH1	1 Orbital sanding machine	16.25	2.43	18.68
		Reason: faulty mechanism. Replacement not requested. credit note issued 1/10/85						

Credit note issued by supplier for returned goods

Credit Note C223

Greendyke Tools

Greendyke Limited,
Worthing Lane
Manchester M32 T5

Telephone: 061 8218001
VAT Reg. No: 223-3269-92

J.R. Hyland
Joinery & Hardware Stores
6 Treelane Avenue
Old Felton
GATESHEAD, Tyne & Wear NE8 3L

Date/Tax Point 1/10/85

Goods by: Road ☐
　　　　　Rail ☐
　　　　　Post ☐

Goods Received: **Faulty**

Quantity	Description Price	Amount excluding VAT	VAT Rate	VAT Net
1	Orbital Sander T632-2	16.25	15%	2.43
		16.25		2.43
	VAT	2.43		
	Total	£18.68		

ROB1/1

Posting of credit note in the ledger

LEDGER

DR							CR
Date	Details	Folio	£ p	Date	Details	Folio	£ p
			Greendyke Tools G1				
1985							
Oct. 1	Credit note	ROB1	16.25				
✓	VAT	ROB1	2.43				
				VAT A/C V1			
				1985			
				Oct. 1	Credit note	ROB1	2.43

Discount received and VAT

Cash discount is an allowance which a business owner sometimes makes to customers who pay their bills promptly. It means that the customers have a small percentage deducted from the total amount due. The treatment of discount received with regard to VAT is shown overleaf.

J.R. Hyland received the following invoice on August 13, 1985.

Sales invoice from Hadrian Supply Company to J.R. Hyland Joinery and Hardware Stores

Sales Invoice

Invoice No. 326H9

Telephone: 061-29510
Date: 12th August 1985
Terms: 2½% - 7 days.

Beaufort Street
Newcastle-upon-Tyne
NE2 6Q

Hadrian Supply Company

To

J.R. Hyland Joinery & Hardware Stores
7 Treelane Avenue
Old Felton,
GATESHEAD, Tyne & Wear NE8 3L

Ref. No. Quantity	Description and Price per Unit		Amount Exclusive of VAT	VAT Rate	VAT Net
CAL 99					
3	Bathroom cabinets	25.50	76.50	15%	11.47
CAL 15					
1	Dark glass shelf 12" × 5"	9.99	9.99	15%	1.50
			86.49		12.97
		VAT	12.97		
			£99.46		

He took advantage of the 2½% discount offered and paid the account on August 14, 1985. This is how he calculated the input VAT:

Cost price	86.49	
Less 2½%	2.16	84.33
Add VAT at 15%		12.64
Amount due with discount:		£96.97

He therefore paid a cheque to Hadrian Supply Company for £96.97.

The cash book entry for this payment was:

Entry of payment with discount received in cash book

CASH BOOK CB2 (Payments side)							
Date	Details	Folio	Discount Received	Input VAT	Net	Cash	Bank
1985							
Aug. 14	Hadrian Supply Co	H1	2.16				96.97

The entries in J.R. Hyland's ledger for Hadrian Supply Company were:

Posting of entries in the ledger of J.R. Hyland

LEDGER							
DR							**CR**
Date	Details	Folio	£ p	Date	Details	Folio	£ p
			Hadrian Supply Co. H1				
1985				**1985**			
Aug. 14	Bank	CB2	96.97	Aug. 5	Purchases	PDB1	86.49
	Discount	CB2	2.16	✓ 5	VAT	PDB1	12.97
✓ 14	Balance to VAT Account		0.33				
			99.46				99.46
			VAT Account V1				
1985				**1985**			
Aug. 5	Purchases	PDB1	12.97	Aug. 14	Hadrian Supply Co.	H1	0.33

Discount allowed and VAT

J.R. Hyland issued the following invoice to a credit customer and allowed $2\frac{1}{2}\%$ discount for prompt payment.

Sales invoice from J.R. Hyland offering discount

J R Hyland

JOINERY & HARDWARE STORES

Invoice/Job No 79

6 Treelane Avenue, Old Felton, Gateshead, Tyne and Wear, NE8 3L.   Telephone 091 361200

VAT Reg No 23-9620-80
Date: 4th Sept. 1985

R. McGivern
Oakhill
North Oakhill Park
DUNSTON, Tyne & Wear NE7 2T

Quantity	Description	Price per Pack	Amount	VAT Rate	VAT Net
40	Ceramic Tiles 6 × 6 × 3/16 (Avocado) Packs of 10	8.50	340.00	15%	51.00
20	Ceramic Tiles (Patterned) Packs of 10	8.75	175.00	15%	26.25
			515.00		77.25
		VAT	77.25		
		Total	592.25		

Terms: 2½% – 10 days

R. McGivern paid his account on September 8, 1985. This is how he calculated the amount due:

Total cost price	515.00	
Less 2½%	12.87	502.13
Add VAT at 15%	——	75.31
Amount due with discount:		£577.44

The cash book entry for this discount in J.R. Hyland's book was:

Entry of discount allowed in the cash book

DR				CASH BOOK (Receipts side)				
Date	Details	Folio	Discount Allowed	Output VAT	Net	Cash	Bank
1985							
Sept. 8	R. McGivern	McG1	12.87				577.44

The ledger entry for R. McGivern's account was:

Posting of discount allowed in customer's account in the ledger

			LEDGER				
DR							**CR**
Date	Details	Folio	£ p	Date	Details	Folio	£ p
			R. McGivern McG1				
1985				1985			
Sept. 8	Sales	SDB1	515.00	Sept. 8	Bank	CB2	577.44
✓ 8	VAT	SDB1	77.25	✓ 8	Discount	CB2	12.87
				✓ 8	Balance trans. to VAT account		1.94
			£592.25				£592.25

The adjustment in the VAT account was:

Adjustment of VAT account in the ledger for discount allowed

			LEDGER				
DR							**CR**
Date	Details	Folio	£ p	Date	Details	Folio	£ p
			VAT Account V1				
1985							
Sept. 8	R. McGivern	McG.1	1.94				

Trade discount

Cash discount is recorded in the cash book as either discount allowed or discount received. It must be always posted to the ledger. Trade discount does *not* appear in either the cash book or the ledger because it is quite different. It is a reduction in the listed price of an article given by manufacturers to traders to enable them to make an extra profit.

> Trade discount is recorded in the purchases day book only and never in the ledger.

Below is an example of a VAT invoice with trade discount having been deducted. Note that the VAT charge has been added to the net price of £9.75.

Sales invoice showing trade discount

INVOICE   PDB1/1

Yardley Repro Supplies Ltd.

High Street, Liverpool L5 7PC
Telephone: 051-210 5375

Our Invoice No. 281
Your Ref. TR62
Vat Reg. No 063–39–61   Date: November 6, 1985

To: T. Robinson
   3 High Street, Hull HU1 3FQ

	Price Per Unit	Price	VAT
2 × 5 litre blanket wash	£3.50	£7.00	@ 15%
1 litre preserving solution	1.75	1.75	
1 litre fixing solution	1.50	1.50	
		10.25	
Less trade discount		0.50	
		£9.75	1.46
	Plus VAT	1.46	
		£11.21	

Terms: Net 1 month

Carriage in/carriage out and VAT

Invoices which show charges for carriage in/carriage out by road, rail, sea or air are subject to VAT.

For example, suppose Greendyke Tools delivered the goods referred to in their invoice on page 25 by road to J.R. Hyland, and charged carriage of £15.00.

The invoice would then read:

Extract from sales invoice to show adjustments for carriage

	Amount excluding VAT	VAT Rate	VAT Net
	212.97	15%	31.94
Carriage	15.00		2.25
Total	227.97		
Plus VAT at 15%	34.19		
	£262.16		£34.19

The petty cash book and VAT

Petty cash book rulings for VAT

PETTY CASH BOOK											
RECEIPTS					PAYMENTS						
£	p	Folio	Date	Details	Voucher No.	Total	Input VAT	Travel	Postage	Cleaning	Stationery	Purchases Sundries

Each column in the petty cash book is totalled at the end of the week, or month, whichever is applicable. The *total* of each column is posted to the **ledger account**, and not the individual items.

Sundry purchases and stationery etc. are subject to 15% VAT. They are posted to the ledger in the usual way, and a VAT input account is also opened in the ledger.

N.B. The treatment of VAT in the final accounts is included in Chapter 9, 14 and 16.

Chapter 3 Exercises

Purchases and VAT

1 *The Scribe Shop received the following invoices for the month of December, 1985. You are asked to enter them in the purchases day book PDB1 using the column headings shown on page 27.*

- *Number the invoices in the invoice column and post each entry into the ledger, using the traditional "T" method.*
- *Open a VAT account.*
- *Open a purchases account.*

Bought from Charlton Stein & Co.:

Dec. 1 5 sets cartography pens at £2.50 per set.
5 sets calligraphy pens at £4.99 per set.

Dec. 10 10 sets watch pens at £2.50 per set.

Dec. 14 4 ballpoint fountain pens, gift box packed, at £6.50 per pack.
2 document cases at £9.75 each.

All the above invoices are subject to standard rate VAT at 15%.

2 *Enter the following invoices in the purchases day book (PDB2) of W. Wentworth.*

- *Post the entries to the ledger in the appropriate accounts using the traditional "T" method.*
- *Open a VAT account.*
- *Open a purchases account.*

1986
Jan. 10 Bought from Centaur Office Supplies:

1 Meadway portable typewriter, elite typeface, 12″ carriage	£39.00
1 Meadway electric typewriter, pica typeface, 18″ carriage	£165.90
1 Clayton Instruments calculator	£8.50
1 Clayton desk top school calculator	£12.00
1 Clayton electronic calculator	£14.75

The costs of the above purchases are subject to 15% VAT.

Cash purchases with VAT

1 *On January 4, 1986 Melissa Boutique purchased sundry items and paid by cash £230.00 plus 15% VAT. Show the entry in the cash book (CB12) and make the appropriate ledger entries.*

2 *On February 10, 1986 R. Croyte purchased stock at a bankruptcy sale for £250.36 plus VAT at 15%, paid by cash.*

Show the entry in Croyte's cash book (CB13) and make the necessary entry in the ledger accounts.

Sales and VAT

1 *Sparkle & Shine Industrial Cleaners issued the following invoices for the month of December, 1985. You are asked to enter them in the sales day book (SDB4) using the column headings shown on page 33.*

- *Enter the job number.*
- *Number the invoices in the invoice column and post the entries into the ledger using the running balance style as shown on page 29.*
- *Open a VAT account for December 31, 1985.*
- *Open a sales account.*

Dec. 3 Job 122, *Charlton Fraser Limited*: interior and exterior windows
and entrance porch cleaned £142.56 + VAT
Job 123, *The Central Office Block*:
exterior window cleaning £1,149.20 + VAT
Dec. 15 Job 127, *Fraser Jordan & Partners*: carpets
and curtains cleaned and repaired £1,515.88 + VAT
Dec. 19 Job 128, *Bali Secretarial School*:
window cleaning £149.20 + VAT
classroom partitions £75.00 + VAT

2 *Aladdin's Cave Soft Toy Manufacturers issued the following invoices for the credit sales for the month of December 1985.*

- *Number and enter the invoices in the sales day book (SDB5) using the rulings on page 33.*
- *Post the entries to the ledger (using the running balance style).*
- *Open an output VAT account for December 31, 1985.*
- *Open a sales account.*

1985

Dec. 5   *Tinsel Town Toy Shop:*
12 teddy bears 14″ at £15.00 each.
10 yapping puppies at £10.00 each.
6 remote control kittens at £8.50 each.
20 mama dolls at £9.75 each.
All the above are subject to 15% VAT.

Dec. 10   *The Dolly Mixture Toy Shop:*
30 baby dolls at £10.00 each.
30 rag dolls at £10.00 each.
All the above are subject to 15% VAT.

Dec. 10   *R. Croyte:*
24 cuddly rabbits at £12.75 each.
12 lion cubs at £15.55 each.
All the above are subject to 15% VAT.

Cash sales with VAT

1 *On January 5, 1986 T. Bjorg Sports Wear Manufacturer's cash sales amounted to £3,998.34 which included 15% VAT. Show the entry in the cash book (CB11), the sales account and the output VAT account.*

2 *On January 30, 1986 Melissa Boutique's till receipts (cash sales) for the month amounted to £525.75 which included 15% VAT. Show the cash book (CB12), the sales account and the output VAT account for the month.*

Returns inward and VAT

1 On December 5, 1985 Aladdin's Cave Soft Toy Manufacturers sold (SDB1) 20 mama dolls at £9.75 each plus 15% VAT to Tinsel Town Toy Shop.

On December 12, 1985 Tinsel Town Toy Shop returned 5 dolls because they were damaged.

On December 13, 1985 Aladdin's Cave sent a credit note for the returned goods.

Show the entries in Aladdin's Cave Soft Toy Manufacturers' books to record the transaction using the traditional "T" method in the ledger.

2 On December 4, 1985 T. Bjorg Sports Wear Manufacturer sold (SBD6) 20 sets of tungsten darts at £10.52 plus 15% VAT per set to Parkside Sports and Leisure Centre.

On December 11 Parkside Sports and Leisure Centre returned 2 sets, the flights being out of alignment.

On December 12 T. Bjorg Sports Wear issued a credit note for the faulty goods.

Show the entries in T. Bjorg Sports Wear's records for these transactions using the traditional "T" method in the ledger.

Returns outward and VAT

1 On December 10, 1985 the Scribe Shop purchased 10 sets of watch pens at £2.50 per set plust 15% VAT from Charlton Stein & Co. On December 15 they returned 4 sets as being faulty. Charlton Stein & Co. sent a credit note to the Scribe Shop the same day.

Show the entries for this credit in the Scribe Shop's returns outward book (ROB6) and the necessary ledger entries, using the traditional "T" method.

2 On January 15, 1986 Snip-It Unisex Hairdressers purchased from Moderna Hairdressing Supplies ten sets of hair trimmers and scissors at £32.50 per set plus 15% VAT. Two pairs of scissors were not the same as ordered.

On February 2, 1986 Moderna Hairdressing Supplies sent a credit note for the full amount.

- *Show the entries in Snip-It Unisex Hairdressers' returns outward book (ROB2) and ledger accounts, using the traditional "T" method.*
- *Show the entries in Moderna Hairdressing Supplies' returns inward book (RIB2).*

Discount received and VAT

1 On February 28, 1986 R. Tighe bought goods (PDB1) valued at £135.50 plus 15% VAT from M. Badat. He deducted $2\frac{1}{2}$% discount and paid by cheque on March 2, 1986.

- *Show the calculations and the amount R. Tighe has gained by receiving the discount.*
- *Show the cash book (CB6) and ledger entries for the transaction.*

2 On March 28, T. Roberts bought goods from T. Corrigan. The invoice total was £698.00 plus 15% VAT. He was allowed a discount of $3\frac{1}{2}$% and paid by cheque on April 2, 1986 (CB10).

Show the calculations required for the cash book and ledger entries.

Discount allowed and VAT

1 On October 21, 1985 C. Hui sold goods for cash valued at £21.00 plus 15% VAT. He gave a discount of $2\frac{1}{2}\%$ for cash payment.

Make the cash book (CB2) and ledger entries.

2 On October 15, 1985 C. Hui sold goods on credit to S. Arbuthnot for £435.00 plus 15% VAT, allowing him a discount of $3\frac{3}{4}\%$ S. Arbuthnot paid by cheque on October 20, 1985.

Make the cash book (CB2) and ledger entries for this transaction.

Answers are given in the Worked Solutions.

4 The Balance Sheet

In Chapters 1 and 2 we extracted from Tom Robinson's trial balance those figures which are necessary to make up his trading account and profit and loss account. These are Tom's final accounts, and all of the relevant accounts have now been 'closed' in the ledger.

There are still a number of balances remaining 'open', as shown in the following extract from the trial balance.

Extract from Tom's trial balance

		Debit Balances	Credit Balances
Cash in hand	CB3	161.88	
Cash at bank (overdrawn)	CB3		104.88
Baker T.	B1		25.00
Black T.	B3		75.00
Blake Forest T.	B4		36.00
Brown L.	B5		12.00
Brunetti R.	B6		51.25
Gregg C.	G1		40.00
Ho T.	H1	123.00	
Johnson J.	J1	36.20	
Lawson K.	L1	50.00	
Mark J.	M2		25.00
Paper Mill Ltd	PM1	25.00	
Rowell Forwarding Co.	R3	15.00	
Walker W.	W3		60.00
Wilson R.	W2	102.50	
Capital	CA1		800.00
Machinery	M1	284.00	
Petty cash account	PC1	50.00	
Van	SA1	450.00	
Drawings account	DA1	30.00	

Stock unsold @ Dec. 31, 1985   £115.00

These items are now going to be recorded in a new form of trial balance which is called the balance sheet. It differs from the full trial balance because it only contains a list of those items which are the **assets** or **liabilities** of a firm *as at a certain time*. The heading therefore is:

BALANCE SHEET

As at . . . . 19. . .

and *never* 'for the year (or other period) ended'.

They are being transferred from the ledger to the balance sheet because the balance sheet is *not* an account, even though it is the concluding section of the final accounts.

> The balance sheet is a **statement** and does not have a Dr and Cr side. The totals on either side of this statement must agree, and so it does not show an amount left over to form a balance, as does an account.

The definitions of assets and liabilities are to be found in Volume 1, Chapter 10.

The assets

Using ledger paper we will now prepare the assets side of Tom's balance sheet. The various sections will be explained afterwards on page 59.

Assets side of Tom's balance sheet

T. ROBINSON			BALANCE SHEET					
			as at December 31, 1985					
Date	Details		£	p	Date	Details	£	p
	LIABILITIES					ASSETS		
						Fixed assets		
						Machinery 284·00		
						Van 450·00	734	00
						Current assets		
						Stock unsold at 31·12·1985	115	00
						Debtors		
						T. Ho 123·00		
						J. Johnson 36·20		
						K. Lawson 50·00		
						Paper Mill Ltd 25·00		
						Rowell Finding 15·00		
						R. Wilson 102·50	351	70
						Cash in hand 161·88		
						Petty cash 50·00	211	88
							£1412	58

We learned in Chapter 10 of Volume 1 that assets are the property and possessions of a business. As such they should be clearly grouped under one of two headings in the balance sheet so that the owner can see at a glance the value of each group.

Fixed assets

Fixed assets are assets which have been purchased and which the owner intends to keep in the firm more or less permanently. In Tom's case he needs machines to produce goods for various printing orders from his customers, and needs the van to collect the work and deliver the finished products. His business could not exist without them.

Current assets

Current assets (so called from the French word 'courant' meaning 'running' – sometimes called 'circulating assets') are assets which are destined to be sold and changed into cash. Tom has 'cash' with which he will buy stock to sell to his customers (his **debtors**). When the customers pay him, they will give him more 'cash' to buy more stock. The circle will then go round again, keeping the system running.

It is important to list the current assets as shown in the balance sheet on page 58.

1) *Stock.* This is the stock unsold at December 31, 1985, value £115, which is shown on page 1. It is an asset because it is available for sale at a profit.

2) *Debtors.* These are customers who will be due to pay their outstanding monies to Tom within the immediate future (possibly within the month).

    Although the individual accounts in Tom's balance sheet have been listed in order to copy the items from his new trial balance, in practice the amounts would be totalled, and shown as one figure:
    Debtors   £351.70

3) *Cash and petty cash.* Likewise these two items would be shown as one:
    £161.88 + £50 = £211.88

The liabilities

We will now prepare the liabilities side of Tom's balance sheet. Again, the various sections will be explained afterwards on page 61.

Liabilities side of Tom's balance sheet

Date	Details		£	p	Date	Details		£	p
	T. ROBINSON		BALANCE SHEET						
			as at December 31, 1985						
	LIABILITIES					ASSETS			
	Capital		800	00					
Add	Net profit		213	45					
			1,013	45					
Less	Drawings		30	00					
			983	45					
	Current liabilities								
	Creditors:								
T. Baker		25·00							
T. Black		75·00							
T. Blake Forest		36·00							
L. Brown		12·00							
T. Gregg		40·00							
J. Mark		25·00							
R. Brunetti		51·25							
W. Walker		60·00	324	25					
	Bank overdraft		104	88					
			£1412	58					

Capital

1) **Capital** is the difference between the assets and liabilities. An explanation of this was given in Chapter 10 of Volume 1. Tom's capital of £800 was the amount he invested on September 1, 1985.

2) **Net profit** is the figure brought from the profit and loss account and is added to the capital. The way we arrived at this figure is shown on pages 18-19.

   On the other hand, if the profit and loss account has shown a **net loss** instead of a net profit then the amount of the loss would have been *deducted* from the capital.

Drawings

From the combined capital and net profit we must deduct the money which Tom has drawn for his personal use during the period. These **drawings** reduce the liability of the firm to him as its owner. (Remember the business and its owner are separate entities. The business *owes* Tom his livelihood.)

Current liabilities

1) **Creditors** are people Tom owes money to, such as his suppliers. He will be expected to pay this money due to them within the immediate future (that is, one month).

   As with the current assets, the accounts for these creditors are usually shown as a single total.

2) **Bank overdraft** is the amount Tom owes his bank (£104.88). It will have to be repaid within the agreed time.

> If Tom's account at the bank was *not* overdrawn then his credit balance would be included in the *current assets* in the following order:
>
> - Stock
> - Debtors
> - Bank
> - Cash in hand

The balance sheet

We shall now combine the left- and right-hand sides of the balance sheet in the traditional or horizontal style.

Traditional (horizontal) presentation of Tom's balance sheet

T. ROBINSON
BALANCE SHEET
As at December 31, 1985

LIABILITIES	£	£	ASSETS	£	£
Capital	800.00		Fixed assets		
Add Net profit	213.45		Machinery	284.00	
			Van	450.00	734.00
	1,013.45				
Less Drawings	30.00	983.45	Current assets		
			Stock at 31/12/1985	115.00	
Current liabilities			Debtors	351.70	
Sundry creditors		324.25	Cash	211.88	678.58
Bank overdraft		104.88			
		£1,412.58			£1,412.58

There is another style for presenting this balance sheet. This is called the 'vertical' style and is used in many modern businesses. Tom's balance sheet is given in the 'vertical' style on page 63.

Some examining boards require a certain style or offer a choice, so it is advisable for a candidate to be familiar with both forms. (See also Chapter 18 for further examples of the vertical style of balance sheet.)

Alternative (vertical) presentation of Tom's balance sheet

T. ROBINSON

BALANCE SHEET as at December 31, 1985

ASSETS

	£	£	
Fixed assets			
Machinery	284.00		
Van	450.00	734.00	
Current assets			
Stock at December 31, 1985	115.00		
Debtors	351.70		
Cash in hand	211.88	678.58	£1,412.58

LIABILITIES

Capital	800.00		
Add Net profit	213.45		
	1,013.45		
Less Drawings	30.00	983.45	
Current liabilities			
Sundry creditors	324.25		
Bank overdraft	104.88	429.13	£1,412.58

Chapter 4 Exercises

The balance sheet

1 *Prepare a balance sheet from the following extracts from Belinda Beetle's records:*

Net profit for the year ended January 31, 1986	£2,000
Capital at start	£18,000
Premises	£6,900
Machines	£2,500
Vans	£3,200
Drawings	£1,800
Creditors	£1,700
Bank overdraft	£60
Stock in hand	£1,560
Debtors	£5,500
Cash in hand	£300

2 *From the following information prepare Leslie Carr's balance sheet as at April 30, 1986:*

Capital	£12,647
Net profit for the year	£8,928
Drawings	£1,900
Creditors	£5,789
Furniture	£2,670
Motor cars	£6,000
Stock in hand	£7,954
Debtors	£6,320
Cash at bank	£2,500
Cash in hand	£20

3 *The Wonderland Toy Shop's balance sheet is to be prepared from the following extract from the trial balance for the year ended December 31, 1985:*

Capital at start	£15,545
Net profit for the year	£4,390
Creditors	£3,140
Debtors	£4,500
Stock in hand	£1,000
Cash at bank	£2,025
Premises	£8,200
Display counters and furniture	£2,800
Drawings	£4,550

Answers are given in the *Worked Solutions.*

5 Year-end Adjustments

In Volume 1 we covered all the procedures for double-entry book-keeping for all records for the first four months of Tom Robinson's business, up to the extraction of a trial balance. In Chapters 1, 2 and 4 of this volume we have prepared, in a very simplified form, the final accounts from that trial balance. Since Tom's business is still very small we will leave it for a later chapter to consider his expansion.

However, you will find that typical examination questions involve many more items in businesses which have been established for a number of years. So that we can look at some of these other items in more detail let us consider the following trial balance for Chic Knitwear, covering instead a complete year's trading: September 1, 1985 to August 31, 1986.

From this trial balance we will prepare:

- the trading account
- the profit and loss account
- the balance sheet.

Chic Knitwear trial balance for a complete year's trading

CHIC KNITWEAR

TRIAL BALANCE

Year ended August 31, 1986

	£		£
Cash in hand	80		
Cash at bank	500		
Stock in hand at start of the year	3,000		
Premises	2,600		
Van	1,250		
Knitting machines A/c	500		
Total debtors	2,390		
Total creditors			2,400
Bad debts*	290		
Sales			16,850
Returns (inward)	200		
Purchases	8,600		
Returns (outward)			110
Discount allowed	200		
Discount received			150
Carriage in (purchases)	300		
Carriage out (sales)	470		
Sundry expenses	400		
Rent	240		
Salaries	1,470		
Wages	2,890		
Drawings	1,130		
Capital			7,000
	£26,510		£26,510

In addition to the figures given in the trial balance above we have the following information (called **adjustments**):

	£
● The value of stock in hand at August 31	4,000
● Depreciation:	
1) Vans	100
2) Knitting machines	80
● Payments in arrears:	
1) Wages	70
2) Salaries	40
● Payments in advance – rent	20

Before we can prepare the final accounts we must first consider the information we have been given in more detail.

*See page 67.

Bad debts

The trial balance shows a debit balance of £290 *bad debts*. (You will recall from Chapter 2, page 21, that bad debts occur when goods have been sold but payment is long overdue. Here we will deal with such debts more fully.) This is made up as follows:

- One customer, Mr C. Bird, owes £100. He cannot be traced at all.
- Another customer, W. Waite, owes £280. He was unable to pay, and after he was taken to court (and was declared bankrupt) the court agreed he need only pay £90 as his payment in full. (The loss therefore in this case is £190.)

The following ledger entries show how the position with C. Bird and W. Waite has been recorded in the books of Chic Knitwear.

Chic Knitwear ledger entries to record bad debts

LEDGER										
DR										**CR**
Date		Details	Folio	£	p	Date	Details	Folio	£	p
		C. BIRD		B6						
1985 Sept.	1	Balance	b/d	£100	00	1986 Aug. 31	Trans. to bad debts A/c	BD4	£100	00
		W. WAITE		W3						
1985 Sept.	1	Balance	b/d	280	00	1985 Nov. 30	Bank	CB4	90	00
						1986 Aug. 31	Bad debts trans. to bad debts A/c	BD4	190	00
				£280	00				£280	00
		BAD DEBTS A/c		BD4						
1986 Aug.	31	C. Bird	B6	100	00	Aug. 31	Profit + Loss A/c		290	00
Aug.	31	W. Waite	W3	190	00					
				£290	00				£290	00
		PROFIT + LOSS ACCOUNT								
		year ended August 31, 1986								
		Bad debts		290	00					

It will be seen that the ledger accounts for C. Bird and W. Waite are closed and the total losses of £290.00 are now shown in the profit and loss account as bad debts of £290.00.

Adjustments

These are the items given in addition to those contained in the trial balance. From this information an amount is worked out which must either be added to or subtracted from the figures in the trial balance in order to show the true figure in the final accounts.

Stock unsold at August 31, 1986 (£4,000)

We have already dealt with this in the previous chapter on page 59. It is to be *deducted* from the 'cost of goods sold' in the trading account, and will appear as a *current asset* in the balance sheet.

Depreciation

This is the 'wearing away' of an asset. Premises, vans, machinery, fixtures and fittings are all subject to **depreciation**.

For example, let us say that a second-hand van was bought at the start of the business in September 1985. It cost £450. It has been used consistently for the year. Parts are worn, perhaps replacements have been made, and the mileage will be high too. It is still valuable to the business but it has lost its original market value. This 'loss' caused by the use of an asset is called depreciation.

The amount of the depreciation (or the loss) must be given a **book value** in order that a true picture of the fixed assets may be seen in the balance sheet. (Remember that this is a statement which shows the overall value of the business.)

The calculation of depreciation is a very complicated part of book-keeping. It is sufficient in this beginner's course for you to know the following methods used in modern business:

- the **equal instalments method** (also known as the **straight line method**).
- the **diminishing balance method**.
- **revaluation of constantly changing assets**.

1 Depreciation by the equal instalments method

Suppose on September 1, 1985, a van cost £1,250. It is reckoned that because it will be constantly used it will need to be replaced in 5 years' time, when it is estimated it can be traded in for £750.

To arrive at the loss by equal amounts we use this formula:

$$\text{Cost} = \text{Purchase price} - \text{Selling price} \div \text{Number of years' use}$$
$$= £1,250 - £750 \div 5$$
$$= 500 \div 5$$
$$= £100 \text{ per year}$$

The motor van account will be depreciated by 5 equal instalments of £100.00 and so be reduced to a book value of £750. The motor van account will look like this for the present financial year:

Ledger entry to record depreciation by the equal instalment method

LEDGER

DR										CR
Date		Details	Folio	£	p	Date		Details	Folio	£	p
			MOTOR VAN		ACCOUNT	MV1					
Year 1						Year 1					
1985 Sept.	1	ABC Garage	CB1	1,250	00	1986 Aug.	31	Depreciation A/c	DA1	100	00
						Aug.	31	Balance	c/d	1,150	00
				£1,250	00					£1,250	00
Year 2											
1986 Sept.	1	Balance	b/d	1,150	00						

This will continue each year until the balance has been reduced at Year 5 to £750. The van will then, it is hoped, be traded in for a new one.

The depreciation will also be shown in the appropriate depreciation account and in the profit and loss account.

Ledger entry in the depreciation account

LEDGER

DR										CR
Date		Details	Folio	£	p	Date		Details	Folio	£	p
			MOTOR VAN		DEPRECIATION ACCOUNT D6						
1986 Aug.	31	Motor van	MV1	100	00						

2 Depreciation by the diminishing balance method

This method is very much simpler. The firm decides on a certain percentage to be deducted from the balance outstanding at the end of the year.

Suppose, as above, the van account shows a balance of £1,250 at the end of the financial year. It is decided to write off 20% of the balance outstanding at that time. The van account will show this loss as follows.

Ledger entry to record depreciation by the diminishing balance method

LEDGER												
DR												**CR**
Date		Details	Folio	£	p	Date		Details	Folio	£	p	
			MOTOR VAN			ACCOUNT	MV1					
Year	1					Year	1					
1985 Sept.	1	ABC Garage	CB1	1,250	00	1986 Aug.	31	Depreciation	D6	250	00	
						Aug.	31	Balance	c/d	1,000	00	
				£1,250	00					£1,250	00	
Year	2											
1986 Sept.	1	Balance	b/d	£1,000	00							

At the end of Year 2 this balance of £1,000 will be reduced by a further 20%, £200, making the new balance (the book value of the van) £800.

Again, the depreciation will also be shown in the appropriate depreciation account.

Ledger entry in the depreciation account

LEDGER												
DR												**CR**
Date		Details	Folio	£	p	Date		Details	Folio	£	p	
			MOTOR VAN DEPRECIATION ACCOUNT				D6					
1986 Aug.	31	Motor van	MV1	£250	00							

Depreciation is also shown in the profit and loss account, as given on page 76, which posts the value arrived at using the equal instalment method above.

- The equal instalment method is more appropriate in the case of an asset which has only a relatively short-term life, like a van which is expected to last only a few years.
- The diminishing balance method would be applicable to an asset which is expected to last a greater number of years, the premises or furniture and fittings. If this method is used for an asset such as a van which is expected to last only a short time, a high percentage, say 40%, is necessary to write it off in the books within its expected useful life. This means the profit and loss account would show a disproportionate figure for depreciation in the early years.

3   Revaluation of an asset

Some assets cannot be depreciated by either of the above methods. For example, a sheep farmer cannot put a book value for depreciation on his flock of sheep.

Assets which are constantly changing, like stocks of loose tools, casks, investments, etc., periodically have to be revalued. An inspection by a person who specialises in this type of work is required, and the new valuation is recorded in the books of account.

If, which is quite rare, an appreciation is found, it is *not* generally written in the books.

Let us say, for example, a firm of landscape gardeners has its stock of tools used for forecourt gardening valued by an expert. The book value at January 1, 1986 was £8,000. The new value is estimated on June 30 to be £6,500.

The journal entry would be:

JOURNAL J1					
Date	Details	Folio	Assets	Liabilities	
1986 June 30	Depreciation account	DA1	£1,500.00		
	Tools account	T1		£1,500.00	
	Being decrease in value of forecourt tools as per T. R. Tompkins (Valuers) June 30, 1986				

The ledger entries would be:

LEDGER									
DR									**CR**
Date	Details	Folio	£	p	Date	Details	Folio	£	p
Depreciation Account DA1									
1986 June 30	Tools account	J1	1,500.00						
Tools Account T1									
1986 Jan 1	Balance	b/d	8,000.00		1986 June 30	Depreciation	J1	1,500.00	

Payments in arrears

We will now return to the books of Chic Knitwear. Wages of £70 and salaries of £40 are still outstanding, awaiting payment at August 31, 1986. The business still owes £70 in wages to the employees and is liable to pay this sum. This also applies to the salaries still outstanding.

1) *Wages*
These payments have not been included with the wages (£2,890) shown in the trial balance. Therefore the 'true' figure for wages should read £2,890 + £70 = Wages £2,960. We must therefore show this true figure when we enter the wages in the trading account (see page 75).

We must *also* include £70 in the *current liabilities* in the *balance sheet* (see page 77).

2) *Salaries*
The trial balance shows salaries of £1,470. However, £40 is still outstanding. The true figure for salaries is therefore £1,470 + £40 = £1,510. This must be included in the profit and loss account (See page 76). Remember, £40 must also be shown in the *balance sheet* as a *current liability* (see page 77).

Payments in advance – rent

The total rent paid (£240) covers the period up to September 30. The firm's financial year end is August 31 (as shown by the date of the trial balance). The actual amount of rent due at August 31 was only £220. The £20 has therefore been paid *before* the date it is actually due (paid in advance).

We will show this adjustment in the profit & loss account by a reduction of £20 (see page 76).

Remember, this £20 must also be shown as a *current asset* in the *balance sheet* (see page 77).

Closing entries for adjustments

Before these three adjustments – (wages, salaries and rent) – can be included in the final accounts they must also be entered in the journal and then closed in the ledger, in practice, but this is not normally required in examination questions.

Chic Knitwear journal entries to close wages, salaries and rent accounts

CHIC KNITWEAR	JOURNAL J20			
Date	Details	Folio No.	Assets	Liabilities
1986 Aug. 31	Trading account Dr		2960·00	
	Wages account	W12		2960·00
	Being wages for the year ended August 31, 1986			
Aug. 31	Profit and loss A/c Dr		1,510·00	
	Salaries account	S8		1,510·00
	Being Salaries for the year ended August 31, 1986			
Aug. 31	Profit and loss A/c Dr		220·00	
	Rent account	R6		220·00
	Being rent for the year ended August 31, 1986			

Chic Knitwear ledger closing entries for wages, salaries and rent accounts

CHIC KNITWEAR NOMINAL LEDGER

DR										CR
Date	Details	Folio	£	p	Date	Details	Folio	£	p	
		WAGES	ACCOUNT			W12				
1986 Aug. 1	Total cash	CB16	2,890	00	1986 Aug. 31	Trading account	J20	2,960	00	
Aug. 31	Balance	c/d	70	00						
			2,960	00				2,960	00	
					1986 Sept. 1	Balance	b/d	70	00	
		SALARIES	ACCOUNT S8							
1986 Aug. 1	Total bank	CB16	1,470	00	1986 Aug. 31	Profit + loss A/c	J20	1,510	00	
Aug. 31	Balance	c/d	40	00						
			1,510	00				1,510	00	
					1986 Sept. 1	Balance	b/d	40	00	
		RENT	ACCOUNT R6							
1986 Aug. 1	Total bank	CB16	240	00	1986 Aug. 31	Profit + loss A/c	J20	220	00	
					Aug. 31	Balance	c/d	20	00	
			240	00				240	00	
1986 Sept. 1	Balance	b/d	20	00						

- Payments in arrears must be *added* to the figures given in the trial balance and must appear in *either* the trading account *or* the profit and loss account. They must *always* be shown in the *balance sheet*.
- Payments in advance must always be *subtracted* from the figures given in the trial balance and must appear in *either* the trading account *or* the profit and loss account. They must *always* be included in the *balance sheet*.

The final accounts

We will now return to the trial balance given on page 66 and, entering in all the above adjustments, prepare the final accounts as follows:.

Chic Knitwear trading account

CHIC KNITWEAR

TRADING ACCOUNT

Year ended August 31, 1986

	£	£		£
Stock at			Sales	16,850
September 1, 1985		3,000	Less Returns in	200
Purchases	8,600			
Less Returns out	110	8,490		16,650
		11,490		
Wages	2,890			
Add Wages due*	70	2,960		
		14,450		
Carriage in		300		
		14,750		
Less Stock unsold				
at August 31, 1986*		4,000		
Cost of goods sold		10,750		
Balance being gross profit c/d to profit & loss account		5,900		
		£16,650		£16,650

*These items will also be shown in the balance sheet on page 77.

CHIC KNITWEAR

PROFIT AND LOSS ACCOUNT

Year ended August 31, 1986

	£	£		£
Bad debts		290	Gross profit b/d from	
Discount allowed		200	trading account	5,900
Sundry expenses		400	Discount received	150
Carriage out		470		
Rent	240			
Less Advance*	20	220		
Salaries	1,470			
Add Salaries due*	40	1,510		
Depreciation:				
Vans	100			
Knitting machines	80	180		
Balance being net profit for the year*		2,780		
		£6,050		£6,050

NEVER COUNT YOUR CHICKENS BEFORE THEY'RE HATCHED

*These items are also shown in the balance sheet on page 77.

CHIC KNITWEAR

BALANCE SHEET

as at August 31, 1986

LIABILITIES	£	£	ASSETS	£	£
Capital	7,000		**Fixed assets**		
Add Net profit	2,780		Premises		2,600
	9,780		Vans	1,250	
Less Drawings	1,130	8,650	Less Depreciation	100	1,150
			Knitting machines	500	
			Less Depreciation	80	420
Current liabilities					4,170
Sundry creditors	2,400				
Wages due	70				
Salaries due	40	2,510			
			Current assets		
			Stock unsold	4,000	
			Debtors	2,390	
			Cash at bank	500	
			Cash in hand	80	
			Rent in advance	20	6,990
		£11,160			£11,160

Chapter 5 Exercises

Bad debts

1 Tom Robinson has a customer, C. Carole, who owes him £25. Carole has left the district and cannot be traced. Tom regards this account as a bad debt.
Show the ledger entries for:

- C. Carole's account before and after the transfer to the bad debts account;
- the bad debts account;
- the entry in the profit and loss account.

2 Another customer, D. Davis, owes Tom Robinson £40. The court has declared him to be bankrupt and orders Davis to pay 50p in the pound as a payment in full for his debt.
Show the ledger accounts for:

- D. Davis' account;
- the bad debts account;
- the profit and loss account.

Depreciation

1 On June 2, 1986, Tom Robinson bought a duplicator for £1,800. He estimated that it would be used for 10 years and then be disposed of as useless. The scrap value is estimated to be £200.
Using the equal instalment method, show the machinery account for the first three years.

2 Tom Robinson also has shelving units which cost £800 on June 1, 1986, and which will be depreciated by the diminishing balance method at 10% per annum.
Show the office furniture/fittings account for the first three years.

Revaluation of assets

1 The Display Advertising Company has a quantity of forecourt tools which are constantly in use and wear away fairly quickly. They were valued at £2,000 on January 1, 1985.

Extra tools costing £600 were purchased on March 1.

On December 31 the tool stock was valued at £1,650 by T.R. Johnson.

Show the depreciation by means of a journal entry, and post to the ledger.

2 T. Barrell, a wine merchant, had a stock of casks which were valued at £5,000 on June 1, 1985.

They were revalued by a cooper who estimated that, through fair wear and tear, they had depreciated by £1,500 by June 30, 1986.

Show the journal entry for the depreciation account and the casks account.

3 The Hillsview Poultry Farm has several clutches of Rhode Island Red laying hens valued at £2,000 at January 1, 1986. On June 30, 1986 the Local Farmers' Poultry Assessors' office advised the owners that the flock was now valued at £1,800.

Show the necessary entries in the journal and the ledger for this valuation.

Rent and rates accounts

1 R. Bradshaw rented a room for business premises from M. Crowe at a rent of £325 per quarter payable in arrears.

Bradshaw paid Crowe by cheque on the following dates in 1985: March 30 £325.00; June 30 £325.00; September 30 £325.00.

When Crowe was preparing his profit and loss account, Bradshaw's rent of £325 was still outstanding.

Show the entry in Crowe's ledger

• for Bradshaw's rent account;
• and the profit and loss account.

2 E. Rossini commenced business on January 1, 1985. On January 3 she paid £408 by cheque being rent for three months in advance.

On April 4 she paid six months' rent of £816.

On October 4 she paid £816 being rent up to April 4, 1986.

Show the rent account in E. Rossini's ledger for the year ended December 31, 1985 and the entry in the profit and loss account.

3 W. Wentworth rented premises for £2,800 per year payable quarterly in advance.

The bank account showed the following payments: March 21 £700; June 3 £700; September 6 £700.

Show the rent account in W. Wentworth's ledger for the year ended December 31 and the profit and loss account for that date.

4 *On November 6 a firm paid rates of £2,400 for six months, from November 1, 1985. The profit and loss account was drawn up on December 31, 1985.*

Show the rates account, and profit and loss entries for this transaction.

Final accounts

1

The following trial balance was extracted from the books of Terry Rushworth, butcher, on June 30, 1985.

TRIAL BALANCE
Year ended June 30, 1985

	£	£
Cash in hand	236	
Bank overdraft		2,000
Purchases	16,603	
Till receipts for sales		28,009
Returns inward and outward	320	278
Repairs to equipment	1,508	
Wages	5,000	
Rent	817	
Sundry expenses	407	
Advertising	212	
Painting and decorating	1,244	
Tools and equipment	1,450	
Refrigerators and counters	6,000	
Debtors	1,800	
Drawings	2,000	
Creditors		3,010
Stock at July 1, 1985 (start)	1,700	
Capital		6,000
	39,297	39,297

Using this information:

Show the journal and ledger entries to close the accounts for the following adjustments:

- *the stock in hand at June 30, 1985 was valued at £2,000*
- *wages due but not yet paid to a sales assistant are £40*
- *rent amounting to £57 has been paid in advance*
- *the refrigerators are to be depreciated by 10%*
- *tools and equipment are to be depreciated by £200.*

Prepare a trading account and profit and loss account for the year ended June 30, 1985, together with a balance sheet as at that date. Show each of the adjustments in the appropriate account.

2 The following trial balance was taken from the books of T. McAuley on December 31, 1985.

You are to prepare:

- the trading account for the year ended December 31, 1985.
  The stock unsold at that date was £2,000
- a profit and loss account. The furniture and vans are to be depreciated by 10%
- a balance sheet as at December 31, 1985.

TRIAL BALANCE
Year ended December 31, 1985

	£	£
Stock at January 1, 1985	2,600	
Purchases	36,400	
Returns out		400
Sales		56,000
Wages	6,000	
Salaries	1,000	
Discount allowed	250	
Discount received		100
Electricity A/c	650	
Sundry expenses	1,200	
Debtors	6,400	
Creditors		3,800
Premises	5,000	
Furniture	1,000	
Vans	2,600	
Drawings	2,500	
Cash at bank	1,500	
Cash in hand	600	
Capital		7,400
	£67,700	£67,700

Answers are given in the *Worked Solutions.*

6

Provision for Bad Debts

Every business is likely to have a number of bad debts. During a time when money is scarce (for example, unemployment is high in the area and it is difficult to borrow money from the bank), small businesses are usually the first to be affected as cash cannot be raised to pay the bills. It is therefore prudent for any business to provide, or set aside, from the profit made in one year an amount to compensate for the estimated bad debts in the following year. This amount – the **provision for bad debts** – is decided by taking a fixed percentage of the total debtors shown in the current trial balance.

Recording the provision for bad debts

Let us assume that the trial balance shows the total debtors as £3,400. It could be decided that 5% of this amount would create an appropriate provision for bad debts for the following year:

5% of £3,400 = £170.00

This amount would then be posted in the provision for bad debts account.

In the final accounts the provision for bad debts will appear in the profit & loss account and the balance sheet. The transfer must therefore be shown in:

- the journal
- the profit & loss account (debit side)
- the ledger
- the balance sheet (assets side).

Journal entry to transfer provision for bad debts to profit and loss account

		JOURNAL J3			
Date		Details	Folio No.	Assets	Liabilities
1996 Aug.	31	Profit and loss A/c Dr		170·00	
		Provision for bad debts account			170·00
		Being 5% of Debtors £3400·00 for the year			

Entry for provision for bad debts in profit and loss account

Date	Details	Folio	£	p	Date	Details	Folio	£	p
		PROFIT AND	LOSS	ACCOUNT					
		Year ended	August 31, 1986						
	Provision for bad		170	00					
	debts								

LEDGER — DR / CR

Ledger entry in provision for bad debts account

Date	Details	Folio	£	p	Date	Details	Folio	£	p
	PROVISION FOR BAD	DEBTS ACCOUNT P1							
					1986 Sept. 1	Balance	b/a	170	00

LEDGER — DR / CR

In the balance sheet the provision for bad debts is deducted from the total of the debtors. This will give us the actual amount which should be received in the immediate future.

The balance sheet – assets side

BALANCE SHEET

As at August 31, 1985

LIABILITIES	ASSETS
	Current assets

	£	£
Debtors	3,400	
Less Provision for bad debts	170	3,230

Continuing this example, suppose the trial balance for the next year showed:

Bad debts	£155
Debtors	£6,660

It might well be decided that the provision for this new financial year starting September 1, 1985, will again be 5%, this time of £6,660 = £333.

83

Step 1

We will need to transfer the bad debts (£155) from the ledger to the profit and loss account by means of a journal entry.

Journal entry to close bad debts account

		JOURNAL J3				
Date		**Details**		**Folio No.**	**Assets**	**Liabilities**
1986 Aug.	31	Profit + Loss A/c	Dr		155·00	
		Bad debts A/c		BD1		155·00
		Being transfer of balance to close bad debts				
		account				

The ledger entry will be as follows:

Entry in ledger to close bad debts account

		LEDGER								
DR										**CR**
Date		**Details**	**Folio**	**£**	**p**	**Date**		**Details**	**Folio**	**£**	**p**
		BAD DEBTS		ACCOUNT BD1						
1985 Sept.	1	Sundry debtors	D1	155	00	1986 Aug.	31	Profit + loss A/c		155	00

The profit and loss account entry will be as follows:

Entry of bad debts account in profit and loss account

		LEDGER								
DR										**CR**
Date		**Details**	**Folio**	**£**	**p**	**Date**		**Details**	**Folio**	**£**	**p**
		PROFIT AND		LOSS ACCOUNT						
		Year ended		August 31 1986						
		Bad debts account		155	00						

Step 2

We are now going to show how the new provision for bad debts will appear in the profit and loss account. The credit balance of £170 for the previous year is used again when the new provision for bad debts is calculated.

The *new* provision based on debtors of £6,660 will be:

5% of £6,660	333.00
Less Credit from *old* provision	170.00
	£163.00

Step 3

This £163 must now be shown, as before, in:

- the journal
- the profit and loss account (debit side)
- the ledger.

Journal entry to show new provision for bad debts

	JOURNAL J3			
Date	**Details**	**Folio No.**	**Assets**	**Liabilities**
1986 Aug. 31	Profit + Loss A/c Dr		£163·00	
	Provision for bad debts A/c			£163·00
	Being the additional amount required to raise the provision from £170 to £333 5% of £6,660			

Entry of new provision for bad debts in profit and loss account

	LEDGER								
DR									**CR**
Date	Details	Folio	£	p	Date	Details	Folio	£	p
			PROFIT AND		LOSS	ACCOUNT			
			Year ended		August	31, 1986			
Provision for bad debts (5% × £6,660) New 333·00									
Less	Old 170·00				163	00			

Ledger entry for provision for bad debts account

LEDGER									
DR									**CR**
Date	Details	Folio	£	p	Date	Details	Folio	£	p
	PROVISION FOR BAD DEBTS ACCOUNT P1								
1986 Aug. 31	Balance	c/d	333	00	1985 Sept. 1	Balance	b/d	170	00
					1986 Aug. 31	Profit + Loss A/c		163	00
			£333	00				£333	00
					1986 Sept. 1	Balance	b/d	£333	00

Extract from the balance sheet to show new provision for bad debts

BALANCE SHEET
As at August 31, 1986

LIABILITIES			ASSETS		
			Current assets		
				£	£
			Debtors	6,660	
			Less Provision for bad debts	333	6,327

Preparing the final accounts

Up to this point we have included the ledger entries for the various adjustments before they were entered in the final accounts. Sometimes, an examination question will give a completed trial balance and ask for final accounts to be prepared incorporating the adjustments, without requiring the journal and ledger entries.

We will end this chapter by showing you how to answer such a question. From the following trial balance you are asked to prepare the final accounts, including the adjustments. As a guide the left-hand column shows the relevant account as follows:

- TA – Trading account
- PL – Profit and loss account
- BS – Balance sheet.

Trial balance of P. Stephanou for year ended August 31, 1986

P. STEPHANOU

TRIAL BALANCE

Year ended August 31, 1986

		£	£
(BS)	Capital at September 1, 1986		11,400
(BS)	Drawings	800	
(TA)	Sales		17,390
(TA)	Returns in	80	
(TA)	Purchases	13,856	
(TA)	Returns out		364
(TA)	Wages	1,320	
(PL)	Salaries	2,200	
(PL)	Bad debts	53	
(BS)	Sundry debtors	2,500	
(BS)	Sundry creditors		2,300
(PL)	Discount allowed	200	
(PL)	Discount received		421
(BS)	Premises	2,500	
(BS)	Vans	1,616	
(BS)	Machines	500	
(TA)	Carriage in	268	
(PL)	Carriage out	470	
(PL)	Rates	160	
(PL)	Insurance	120	
(TA)	Stock at start	2,400	
(PL)	Heating & lighting	432	
(PL)	Rent	350	
(BS)	Cash in hand	50	
(BS)	Cash at bank	2,000	
		£31,875	£31,875

Adjustments (see Chapter 5, pages 67-77)

- (TA & BS)   Stock unsold at August 31, 1986, is £3,985.
- (TA/PL & BS) $\frac{2}{5}$ of the rates is to be charged to the profit & loss account. The remaining $\frac{3}{5}$ is for the trading account for the section of premises which is used for production only.
- (PL/BS)   A provision for bad debts is to be created at 5% of the sundry debtors.
- (PL & BS)   An insurance account for £87 is due but not paid.
- (PL & BS)   £50 of the rent paid is in advance.
- (PL & BS)   Depreciate the machinery £50, vans £100.

Trading account of P. Stephanou for year ended August 31, 1986

P. STEPHANOU

TRADING ACCOUNT

Year ended August 31, 1986

	£	£		£
Stock at Sept. 1, 1985		2,400	Sales	17,390
Purchases	13,856		Less Returns in	80
Less Returns out	364	13,492		17,310
		15,892		
Wages		1,320		
		17,212		
Carriage in		268		
		17,480		
Workroom rates $\frac{3}{5} \times$ £160		96		
		17,576		
Less Stock unsold at Aug. 31, 1986		3,985		
Cost of goods sold		13,591		
Balance being gross profit c/d to profit & loss account		3,719		
		£17,310		£17,310

Profit & loss account of P. Stephanou for year ended August 31, 1986

P. STEPHANOU

PROFIT & LOSS ACCOUNT

Year ended August 31, 1986

	£	£		£
Salaries		2,200	Gross profit b/d	
Bad debts		53	from trading account	3,719
			Discount received	421
			Balance being net loss	
Provision for bad debts			c/d to balance sheet	61
5% × £2,500 (Debtors)		125		
Discount allowed		200		
Rates office $\frac{2}{5} \times$ £160		64		
Insurance	£120			
Add Due	87	207		

Heating & lighting		432
Carriage out		470
Rent	£350	
Less Advance	50	300
Depreciation		
Machinery	£50	
Vans	100	150
		£4,201

	£4,201

Balance sheet of P. Stephanou as at August 31, 1986

P. STEPHANOU

BALANCE SHEET

As at August 31, 1986

LIABILITIES	£	£	ASSETS	£	£
Capital	11,400		Fixed assets		
Less Net loss for			Premises		2,500
the year	61		Vans	1,616	
	11,339		Less Depreciation	100	1,516
Less Drawings	800	10,539	Machinery	500	
			Less Depreciation	50	450
					4,466
Current liabilities					
Creditors	2,300				
Insurance due (owing)	87	2,387	Current Assets		
			Stock unsold at		
			Aug. 31, 1986	3,985	
			Debtors 2,500		
			Less Provision		
			for bad debts 125	2,375	
			Cash at bank	2,000	
			Cash in hand	50	
			Rent paid in		
			advance	50	8,460
		£12,926			£12,926

N.B.

In the profit and loss account we created a *new* provision for bad debts.

If, on the other hand, the trial balance had *already* included a debit balance, say:

Provision for bad debts £125

and we were asked to increase the amount to, say, £200, then the entry in the profit and loss account on the debits side would be:

Provision for bad debts	200	
Less Old provision	125	£75

The balance sheet entry would be:

Current assets

Debtors	2,500	
Less Provision for bad debts	200	£2,300

Conversely, if the provision for bad debts was to be *reduced* by £75 then the entry would be:

Provision for bad debts	200	
Less old provision	125	£75
(reduction in provision)		

The balance sheet entry would be:

Current assets

Debtors	2500	
Less Provision for bad debts	125	£2,375

Chapter 6 Exercises

Provision for bad debts

1 *G. Hajee commenced business on January 1, 1985. The debtors for this trading year were £17,000. A provision for bad debts is to be created based on 5% of £17,000.*
Show the provision for bad debts account in G. Hajee's ledger, the profit and loss account and the balance sheet.

2 *The provision for bad debts account shows a credit balance at January 1, 1986, of £200. The new provision is to be increased to £350.*
Show the provision for bad debts account, the profit and loss account and the balance sheet for the year ended December 31, 1985.

3 *The provision for bad debts account in L. Chang's ledger shows a credit balance of £330. This is to be reduced to £250. Show the entry for this transaction:*

- *in the provision for bad debts account*
- *in the profit and loss account*
- *in the balance sheet, where the debtors for the year are to be shown as £5,600.*

Answers are given in the *Worked Solutions.*

7 Interpretation of Final Accounts I

The trading/profit and loss accounts

There are two reasons for preparing these final accounts:

1) to record what has taken place in the previous **trading period** (normally taken as one year, but sometimes may be only part of the year);

2) to reveal any weaknesses, or to show how improvements could be made in the future.

To reveal the weaknesses or show how improvements could be made we compare the figures for one trading period with those of another of the same length, i.e. the figures of the current year with the figures of the previous year. The most useful comparisons which can be made are as follows:

- from the trading account:
    1) the **gross profit percentage on net sales (turnover)**
    2) the **rate of stock turnover**

- from the trading account and also the profit and loss account:
    1) the **percentage of net profit on turnover**
    2) the **percentage of expenses on turnover**

In order to be able to compare the figures of one trading period with another, accuracy in both physically checking and recording the separate items of stock is essential. The 'closing stock' (unsold) at the end of one year, forms the 'opening stock' (stock at start) of the next year. This can be seen from the following two trading accounts for successive years.

Examples of trading accounts for successive years to show relationship of closing stock of Year 1 to opening stock of Year 2

Year 1		TRADING ACCOUNT			
		Year ended December 31, 1984			
	£	£			£
Stock at start		1,500	Sales		28,000
Purchases	12,800		*Less Returns*		400
Less Returns	700	12,100	(Net sales)		27,600
Wages		450			
		14,050			
Less Stock unsold at December 31 1984		**2,000**			
Cost of goods sold		12,050			
Balance being gross profit c/d to profit and loss account		15,550			
		£27,600			£27,600

93

Trading account showing opening stock for year 2

Year 2		TRADING ACCOUNT		
		Year ended December 31, 1985		
	£			£
Stock at start	**2,000**	Sales		55,200
Purchases	22,600			
	24,600			
Wages	500			
	25,100			
Less Stock unsold at December 31, 1985	1,000			
Cost of goods sold	24,100			
Balance being gross profit c/d to profit and loss account	31,100			
	£55,200			£55,200

Gross profit percentage on turnover

We will use the two trading accounts above to find what the gross profit percentage is in relation to the **net sales** for both years. This is also known as the gross profit percentage on turnover. (*Turnover* is the word used by accountants to describe the net sales.)

To calculate this percentage the total amount of the gross profit is divided by the total amount of the net sales (the turnover) and multiplied by 100. For each of the years this will be:

Year 1
- The gross profit is £15,550
- The turnover is £27,600
- Therefore the percentage of gross profit on turnover is:

$$£\frac{15,550}{27,600} \times 100 = 56.34\%$$

Year 2
- The gross profit is £31,100
- The turnover is £55,200
- Therefore the percentage of gross profit on turnover is:

$$£\frac{31,100}{55,200} \times 100 = 56.34\%$$

You will note that the gross profit percentage has remained the same, 56.34%. This is good for the business. If the percentage of gross profit remains constant it enables the owner to estimate the gross profit at regular intervals during the year. The same method of presenting the trading account each year is necessary to make it easy to compare the figures.

However, if the gross profit percentage *decreases* to a noticeable extent then some explanations will be necessary. One reason could be that the stock at the end of the year has been overcharged.

If we look at the trading account for Year 2 we see, quite rightly, that the stock at *start* (£2,000) is the same as the stock *unsold* for Year 1 (£2,000).

Let us assume, however, that a mistake has been made in the figure for the stock unsold at December 31, 1984, in Year 1, which shows £4,000 in error. The trading account for Year 2 would, as a result, look like this:

Trading account showing incorrect figure for stock unsold in previous year

TRADING ACCOUNT

Year ended December 31, 1985

	£		£
Stock at start	4,000	Sales	55,200
Purchases	22,600		
	26,600		
Wages	500		
	27,100		
Less Stock unsold at December 31, 1985	1,000		
Cost of goods sold	26,100		
Balance being gross profit c/d to profit and loss account	29,100		
	£55,200		£55,200

If we now calculate the revised gross profit percentage:

$$\frac{\text{Gross profit}}{\text{Turnover}} \times 100 =$$

$$£\frac{29,100}{55,200} \times 100 = 52.71\%$$

we see that it has in fact *decreased* by 3.63%.

An alternative reason for the decrease could be that cash is being taken from the till dishonestly. The sales figures will fall; so will the gross profit.

On the other hand, perhaps the stock is being damaged by careless handling or storage so that it has to be sold more cheaply. This likewise will reduce the gross profit. Perhaps, too, it is being pilfered.

One very legitimate explanation could be that the cost of the purchases has risen and, because of local competition, the owner has had to delay in passing on the higher costs to the customers.

On the brighter side, a *rise* in the gross profit percentage can be the result of improved efficiency, both by the management and the workers.

Valuation of stock

Stocktaking after the financial year end

In Chapter 1 stock in hand was defined as the stock which is unsold at the end of the trading period. The individual items of stock are physically counted and valued at either the invoice (cost) price or the market price, whichever is the lower.

Very frequently, however, it is not possible for stocktaking to be carried out until some time after the end of the financial year. When this happens an adjustment must be made to make allowance for any purchases or sales which have taken place between the financial year end and the date of stocktaking.

Example 1

The Scribe Shop's year ended on December 31, 1985 but the staff were unable to commence stocktaking until January 6, 1986 when the stock was valued at £2,400. Between January 2 and 6 their suppliers delivered goods amounting to £400 and the shop sold goods valued at £250. The gross profit is 25% on the cost price.

The figure for the value of the stock shown in the balance sheet is calculated as:

	£
Stock figure as per stocktaking January 6	2,400
Less Purchases delivered between December 31, 1985 and January 6, 1986	400
	2,000

		£	
Add	Sales since December 31	250	
Less	25% gross profit on cost	50	200
	Stock at December 31		£1,800

Note: The selling price is £250 and gross profit 25%. Therefore the cost price is

$£250 \times \dfrac{100}{125} = £200.$

Example 2

Here is another example taking into account goods which have been returned inward and outward since the end of the financial year.

W. Wentworth's financial year ended on December 31, 1985 but stocktaking did not commence until January 6, 1986. The stock at that date was valued at £3,475.

Between December 31, 1985 and January 6, 1986 the following transactions took place:

	£
Purchases delivered	240
Goods returned out to suppliers	20
Sales to customers	215
Returns in from sales (selling price)	50

The selling price is 20% on cost price.

Calculate the stock shown in the balance sheet as at December 31, 1985.

		£	£
	Stock value January 6		3,475
Less	Purchases delivered since December 31		240
			3,235
Add	Purchases returned out since December 31		20
			3,255
Add	Goods sold	215	
	Less 20%	43	172
			3,427
Less	Returns in £50 minus 20% (£10)		40
	Stock at December 31		£3,387

Estimation of stock value for insurance claims as a result of loss by fire or burglary

In certain circumstances, such as following a fire or burglary, the value of the stock lost is unknown, and quite often the records too are destroyed. A claim against the insurance must therefore be calculated using the average rate of gross profit as a basis. This can be obtained from the previous year's trading accounts, and the last balance sheet will show the opening stock for the current year. Copies of the final accounts can be obtained from the company's auditors or the Inland Revenue Office.

An estimate of credit sales can also be obtained by contacting customers for sight of their records. Purchases can similarly be estimated from suppliers' records.

The value of any salvaged stock must be deducted from the estimate for the insurance claim.

Worked example

On November 20, 1985 a fire destroyed the stock of timber on the premises of the Timber Wolf Logging Company Limited. The following details were obtained from the accounts:

Stock at cost on December 31, 1984	£12,720
Purchases (January 1–November 20, 1985)	£22,500
Sales (January 1–November 20, 1985)	£30,250
Stock salvaged after the fire	£3,360

The normal gross profit is 28% on cost.

Calculate the amount of the insurance claim for the stock lost.

Model answer

The Timber Wolf Logging Company Limited
Calculation of stock lost by fire November 20, 1985

	£	£
Opening stock		12,720
Purchases (January 1 – November 20 1985)		22,500
		35,220
Less sales (January 1 – November 20 1985)	30,250	
Less 28% gross profit on cost*	6,617	23,633
		11,587
Less salvaged stock		3,360
Insurance loss		8,227

*See formula on page 97.

Rate of stock turnover

We have seen on page 94 that turnover is the net sales of a business (i.e. sales less returns in). We must now find the number of times that the stock has been sold (turned into cash) and replaced by new stock.

In Chapter 3 we saw how the current or circulating assets progress from the selling of *stock* to the *debtors* for *cash* in order to buy more *stock*. Every time this circle is completed a profit should have been made. The rate of stock turnover is the number of times this circle has been completed during a given trading period.

If we say, for example, that the rate of stock turnover is 4, it means that in the course of a year the stock has been sold and replaced four times.

The rate of stock turnover will differ with the kind of stock held by different trades. If a grocer's stock of butter turned over only four times a year then that would not be considered to be a good rate, because butter is a perishable commodity. A newsagent, on the other hand, needs a daily stockturn for newspapers, and perhaps a weekly or monthly stockturn for magazines, whereas a furniture store will be doing well if its stock of beds turns over twice in a year.

Calculating the rate of stock turnover

From the trading account for Year 1 on page 93 we can see the total **cost of goods sold**. If we divide this by the cost of the **average stock**, it will give us the number of times the stock has been sold and replaced.

To find the average stock we add the value of the stock at the *beginning* of the period to that at the *end* of the period and then divide by 2:

	Opening stock	£1,500
Add	Closing stock	£2,000
	Divide	£3,500 by 2 = £1,750

Average stock is therefore £1,750

We can now calculate the rate of stock turnover:

$$\text{Rate} = \frac{\text{Total cost of goods sold}}{\text{Average stock}} = £\frac{12,050}{1,750} = 6.88$$

Rounding this answer up, we would say that the rate of stock turnover was 7.

Percentage of net profit on turnover

We have seen in Chapter 2 that the net profit is the real profit after all the expenses have been deducted from the gross profit.

This net profit can be expressed as a percentage on turnover (net sales) by dividing the net profit by the turnover and multiplying by 100.

Let us assume from a profit and loss account a net profit of £6,000 has been made. Similarly, from the trading account we know that the turnover is £27,600.

Therefore the percentage of net profit on turnover is:

$$\frac{\text{Net profit}}{\text{Turnover}} \times 100 = \frac{6,000}{27,600} \times 100 = 21.73\%$$

As with the gross profit percentage on turnover this should remain a constant figure. A noticeable fall could be caused by a number of factors such as:

- an increase in salaries not in proportion to sales
- a rise in rent or insurances not passed on to the customers
- an increase in bad debts
- advertising costs too great for the results obtained

Percentage of expenses on turnover

In any business individual items of the expenses of that business can vary from period to period. Taking a percentage of an individual item of expense (like salaries) on the turnover of the business is a good way of checking that this expense has not got out of proportion.

We can find the percentage on turnover for each of the expenses in the profit and loss account in the following manner:

$$\frac{\text{Amount of expenses}}{\text{Turnover}} \times 100$$

If we take as an example salaries (this is one expense which is most likely to increase in any business), assuming:

- the profit and loss account gives salaries as £1,500
- the trading account shows turnover to be £27,600

the percentage of salaries on turnover is:

$$£\frac{1,500}{27,600} \times 100 = 5.43\%$$

There are considerable benefits to the owner in knowing the percentage of particular expenses on turnover. If, for example, it is found that the percentage of net profit on turnover (explained above) is showing a decrease on the previous year it will then be possible to see which particular expense(s) need attention.

Worked examination questions

The following questions are typical of those set in examinations. They have been given model solutions to show you how you should approach them.

Question 1

From the following information:

- **a)** prepare a trading account showing the cost of goods sold;
- **b)** show the turnover for the period;
- **c)** show the rate of stock turnover;

100

d) show the gross profit percentage on turnover;

e) if net profit is £8,146, show the percentage of net profit on turnover.

Stock at start (January 1, 1985) £6,500
Stock at finish (December 31, 1985) £7,800
Sales £50,000
Purchases £40,000
Returns inward £1,700
Returns outward £1,700
Wages £200

Model answer

a)

TRADING ACCOUNT
Year ended December 31, 1985

	£	£			£
Stock at start (Jan. 1, 1985)		6,500	Sales		50,000
Purchases	40,000		*Less* Returns in		1,700
					48,300
Less Returns out	1,700	38,300			
		44,800			
Wages		200			
		45,000			
Less Stock at end (Dec. 31, 1985)		7,800			
Cost of goods sold		37,200			
Balance being gross profit c/d to profit and loss A/c		11,100			
		£48,300			£48,300

b) The turnover for the period is £48,300 (net sales).

c) Average stock $= \dfrac{\text{Opening stock} + \text{Closing stock}}{2}$

$$= £\frac{6,500 + 7,800}{2} = £\frac{14,300}{2}$$

$$= £7,150$$

101

$$\text{Cost of goods sold} = £37,200$$

$$\text{Rate of stock turnover} = \frac{\text{Cost of goods sold}}{\text{Average stock}}$$

$$= £\frac{37,200}{7,150}$$

$$= 5.20$$

d) Gross profit percentage on turnover $= \dfrac{\text{Gross profit}}{\text{Turnover}} \times 100$

$$= £\frac{11,100}{48,300} \times 100$$

$$= 22.98\%$$

e) Percentage of net profit to turnover $= \dfrac{\text{Net profit}}{\text{Turnover}} \times 100$

$$= £\frac{8,146}{48,300} \times 100$$

$$= 16.86\%$$

Question 2

From the following information you are asked to show comparisons between the figures for the two trading years of Janice Turner's business.

	Year 1 £	Year 2 £
Turnover	64,000	72,000
Gross profit	15,000	16,000
Net profit	7,000	8,600

Model answer

The gross profit percentage of turnover (net sales):

Year 1: $\dfrac{\text{Gross profit}}{\text{Turnover}} \times 100 = £\dfrac{15,000}{64,000} \times 100 = 23.43\%$

Year 2: $\dfrac{\text{Gross profit}}{\text{Turnover}} \times 100 = £\dfrac{16,000}{72,000} \times 100 = 22.22\%$

The net profit percentage of turnover:

Year 1: $\dfrac{\text{Net profit}}{\text{Turnover}} \times 100 = £\dfrac{7,000}{64,000} \times 100 = 10.93\%$

Year 2: $\dfrac{\text{Net profit}}{\text{Turnover}} \times 100 = £\dfrac{8,600}{72,000} \times 100 = 11.94\%$

Chapter 7 Exercises

Interpretation of final accounts

Study the following accounts for the year ended December 31, 1985 which have been prepared from the books of P. Masterson, and then answer the following questions.

TRADING ACCOUNT						
Year ended December 31, 1985						
		£	£			£
Stock at January 1, 1985			2,655	Sales		31,641
Purchases	20,540					
Less Returns	500		20,040			
			22,695			
Wages			2,500			
Carriage in			120			
			25,315			
Less Stock in hand at December 31, 1985			1,850			
Cost of goods sold			23,465			
Balance being gross profit c/d to profit and loss A/c			8,176			
			£31,641			£31,641

```
            PROFIT AND LOSS ACCOUNT
           Year ended December 31, 1985

                        £                          £
Salaries              1,760   Gross profit b/d   8,176
Advertising             620   Discount received     25
Insurance               100
Discount allowed         90
Repairs and maintenance 630
Rates                   122
Office expenses         152
Balance being net
profit for the year   4,727
                      _____                     _____
                     £8,201                      £8,201
                     ======                      ======
```

1 **a)** *What was the amount of turnover for the year?*
   b) *What was the value of average stock?*
   c) *What was the rate of turnover?*
   d) *What was the gross profit percentage of turnover for the year?*

2 **a)** *What is the net profit percentage of turnover for the year?*
   b) *What is the percentage of the total expenses on turnover?*
   c) *What is the percentage of salaries on turnover?*

Valuation of stock – stocktaking after the financial year end

1 *Jamal Shamji's financial year ended June 30, 1986. Because of a staff shortage stocktaking was not carried out until July 7, 1986 when the stock was valued at £2,662.00.*

Between June 30 and July 7 the following transactions took place:

Goods delivered from suppliers	£98.00
Goods sold to customers	£998.00

Jamal Shamji's business earns a gross profit of 25% on cost price.

From these particulars you are to calculate the true stock figure for June 30, 1986.

2 J.R. Hyland's financial year ended December 31, 1985, but he did not take stock until January 6, 1986. The stock on January 6, 1986 was valued at £6,629.00. Goods valued £662.00 were delivered to him on January 3 and the till receipts showed sales of £2,662.00. The business earned a gross profit of 20% on cost price.

Calculate the stock unsold on December 31, 1985.

3 Aladdin's Cave Soft Toy Shop's financial year ended March 30, 1986. Because this was one of their busiest times – Easter holidays – they were unable to take stock until April 7, 1986. The stock at that date was valued at £2,998.00.

The following transactions took place between the financial year end and the date of stocktaking:

Purchases delivered from supplier	£266.00
Sales	£629.00

Gross profit on cost price is $22\frac{1}{2}\%$.

You are to calculate the value of the stock unsold at March 30, 1986.

4 C. Hui's financial year ended May 31, 1986. It was not possible for his staff to do the stocktaking until June 5, 1986. The stock was valued at £26,953.

Between May 31 and June 5 the following purchases and sales took place:

Purchases delivered from suppliers	£2,300
Sales	£4,600

C. Hui's gross profit is normally 30% on cost price.

Show the value of the stock which would appear as a current asset in the balance sheet as at May 31, 1986.

5 Fashion Accessories' financial year ended August 31, 1986 but the stocktaking was not carried out until September 7 when the stock was valued at £6,953.00.

Between August 31 and September 7 the following transactions took place:

Goods delivered as purchases	£1,720
Goods sold and delivered to customers	£5,369
Goods returned inwards	£80

The firm allows 35% on cost for gross profit.

Calculate the value of the stock at the close of business on August 31, 1986.

6 *T. Bjorg Sports Wear business should have taken stock on May 31, 1986 but owing to pressure of work it was not done until June 9. From the following information you are to calculate the stock in hand at May 31, 1986.*

Stock at June 9	£2,050
Purchases delivered from supplier	
between May 31 and June 9	£125
Sales to customers between May 31 and June 9	£186
Returns inwards between May 31 and June 9	£50

The shop allows 25% on cost for gross profit.

7 *Melissa's Boutique's financial year ended December 31, 1985. The stocktaking did not take place until January 7, 1986, when the stock was valued at £3,000.*

Between December 31 and January 7, 1986 the following deliveries from suppliers and sales to customers took place.

Delivery of purchases from suppliers	£150
Returns outward to suppliers	£62
Goods sold to customers	£300
Returns in from customers	
(selling price)	£85

Melissa's Boutique normally earns a gross profit of 30% on cost price.

Calculate the value of the stock unsold at December 31, 1985.

Estimation of stock value for insurance claims as a result of loss by fire or burglary

1 *On March 21, 1986 there was a burglary at the premises of Panorama Photographs Limited. Stocks of films and processing fluids were stolen.*

From the following records you are to calculate the estimated loss preparatory to the insurance claim:

Stock in hand on December 31, 1985 (figures taken from	
the balance sheet)	£6,629
Purchases (estimated) January 1 to March 21, 1986	£24,653
Sales (estimated) January 1 to March 21, 1986	£16,953
Stock remaining after the burglary	£6,470

The average gross profit on cost price is 35%.

2 *A fire at the premises of the West Oakhill Company Limited on October 10, 1985 destroyed the stock of stationery. A claim was made on the insurance company for the amount of the loss.*

Estimate the amount of this claim from the following particulars:

Opening stock January 1, 1985	£26,953
Purchases from January 1 to October 10, 1985	£12,320
Sales from January 1 to October 10, 1985	£15,661
Salvaged stock estimated value	£7,000

The normal gross profit on cost price is 28%

3 *A fire at the premises of Jamal Shamji on September 19, 1985 destroyed the stock.*

From the following details taken from the accounts calculate the stock loss for the insurance claim:

Stock at December 31, 1985	£11,050
Purchases from January 1 to September 19, 1985	£10,294
Sales from January 1 to September 19, 1985	£18,500
Salvaged stock	£850

Jamal Shamji's mark up on cost price was 25%.

Answers are given in the *Worked Solutions.*

8

Interpretation of Final Accounts II

Examine the following balance sheet. We shall be looking at what it can tell us throughout this chapter.

Example of a balance sheet for analysis

R. JONES

BALANCE SHEET

As at December 31, 1985

LIABILITIES	£	£	ASSETS	£	£	£
Capital at start	25,000		Fixed assets			
Add Net profit	8,100		Premises		9,000	
	33,100		Machines	15,150		
Less Drawings	7,000	26,100	Less			
			Depreciation	150	15,000	
			Vans		4,000	
Long-term liability			Furniture		2,200	30,200
Bank loan (2 years)		10,000				
			Current assets			
Current liabilities			Stock		9,500	
Creditors	5,900		Debtors		4,000	
Bank overdraft	2,000		Cash in hand		250	
Insurance due	50		Rates in			
Wages due	50	8,000	advance		150	13,900
		£44,100				£44,100

Net worth

The **net worth** of the business is the capital. Also called the **capital owned**, it represents the amount of money the owner invested in the business at the start. We add to this the net profit for the year. (Of course if a net loss had occurred then this would reduce the capital.) The net worth of the business represented by the balance sheet above is given on the following page:

Capital	25,000
Add Net profit	8,100
	£33,100
Less Drawings	7,000
Net worth	£26,100

Working capital

The amount of **working capital** in a business is very important. It is the amount of money left over after the fixed assets have been bought and provides money for the day-to-day running expenses of the business. These are, for example, wages and the creditors accounts which fall due within the immediate future.

Working capital is therefore the total of the current assets *minus* the total of the current liabilities.

From the balance sheet on page 108:

The total current assets	13,900
Less The total current liabilities	8,000
Working capital	£ 5,900

(For examples of working capital *included* in the balance sheet see Chapter 18.)

A business should always ensure that it has sufficient working capital in proportion to the total of its fixed assets. If the business has too great a proportion of its capital invested in fixed assets (for example, it has bought an expensive modern machine and there is insufficient demand for its use) then the firm may need to borrow from the bank to pay its immediate commitments (wages, creditors, etc.). The bank will charge interest on the loan (see page 110) which in turn will reduce profits.

If the amount of working capital continues to fall the business will soon fold. It is always necessary, therefore, to ensure that a business has a safe margin of working capital.

Working capital ratio

Accountants have found that the best way to measure the margin of working capital is to work out the ratio of current assets to current liabilities. This is known as the **working capital ratio**. Again using the figures from the balance sheet on page 108:

$$\text{Working capital ratio} = \frac{\text{Current assets}}{\text{Current liabilities}}$$

$$= £\frac{13,900}{8,000}$$

$$= 1.73$$

This ratio could be considered too low (though it would depend on the type of business involved). One explanation would be that the stock is too high (£9,500) since it is more than twice the amount of debtors.

Bank loans and long-term liabilities

If a business borrows money from a bank for any length of time it will be shown in the balance sheet as a **long-term liability**. This is different from a current liability which is due to be paid in the immediate future.

Usually a loan is for a fixed period, such as two years or more, and interest is charged at the rate current when the loan is agreed, and remains at that rate until the loan, plus the interest, is paid back.

Capital employed

The amount of **capital employed** is the total amount of the capital *being used* in the business as at the date of the balance sheet. In any business some of the money which is being used does not belong to that business. It is money owing to the creditors – it has not yet been paid *to* them.

Equally, there is money which *does* belong to the business but is not in use as such because it is being used by the debtors – it has not yet been bid *by* them.

To find the amount of capital employed we find the total value of the assets and subtract the debtors:

Total assets – Debtors = Capital employed

From the balance sheet on page 108:

Money being used:

The owner has supplied	£26,100
The creditors have supplied (£5,900 + £50 + £50)	£ 6,000
The bank has supplied (£10,000 + £2,000)	£12,000
Total assets	£44,100

Money not in use:

The debtors	£4,000

Therefore:

Capital employed = Total assets − Debtors
                 = £44,100 − £4,000
                 = £40,100

The formula for capital employed is:

$$\text{Total value of assets in the balance sheet} - \text{Debtors}$$

Chapter 8 Exercises

The balance sheet

1 *Study the balance sheet below and answer the following questions.*

BALANCE SHEET

As at December 31, 1985

LIABILITIES	£	£	ASSETS	£	£
			Fixed assets		
Capital	15,180		Premises		8,304
Add			Motor vans	4,500	
Net profit	4,727		*Less*		
			Depreciation	450	4,050
	19,907				12,354
Less					
Drawings	1,160	18,747			
Current liabilities			*Current assets*		
Creditors	2,087		Stock in hand	1,860	
			Debtors	6,717	
Bank overdraft	200	2,287	Cash in hand	103	8,680
		£21,034			£21,034

a) *What is the net worth of the business?*
b) *What is the working capital?*
c) *What is the ratio of current assets to current liabilities?*
d) *What is the capital employed?*

2 *From the following details find P. Jones's capital and prepare his balance sheet as at June 30, 1986.*

Stock	£3,740
Debtors	£8,000
Creditors	£6,800
Loan	£300
Wages due	£25
Premises	£11,650
Equipment	£5,200
Vehicles	£5,900
Cash at bank	£11,450

a) *What is the amount of working capital from this balance sheet?*
b) *What is the ratio of current assets to current liabilities?*
c) *Why is the loan called a 'long-term liability' and wages due a 'current liability'?*

3 *From the following balance sheet extracts in the books of Miriam Goldsmith you are asked to do the following:*

a) *Show the working capital for each year.*
b) *Calculate the ratio of current assets to current liabilities.*

	Year 1 £	Year 2 £	Year 3 £
Current assets			
Stock	1,800	1,050	1,266
Debtors	2,080	3,740	2,640
Bank	530	1,500	1,700
Cash in hand	60	180	253
Insurance (pre-paid)	60	–	60
	£4,530	£6,470	£5,919

	£	£	£
Current liabilities:			
Creditors	1,000	1,625	850
Rent due	200	100	200
	£1,200	£1,725	£1,050

Answers are given in the *Worked Solutions.*

9

Further Entries in the Journal

At the end of Chapter 4 we left Tom Robinson's business because it was too small for it to provide us with sufficient examples of the adjustments to and possible interpretations of the final accounts which were covered in Chapters 5–8.

We will now return to Tom's books to consider further aspects of business bookkeeping.

Purchase of assets (including VAT)

As we saw in Volume 1, Chapter 10, assets are the property and possessions of a business.

We have seen that purchases of goods for resale in the business are recorded in either the cash book, when a cash transaction has taken place, or the purchases day book for a credit transaction, before being posted to the ledger (Volume 1, Chapters 6 and 7).

The purchase of *assets*, however, must first be recorded in the journal as the prime book of entry, *whether the asset was paid for by cash or credit*. When the payment is by cash, there will also have to be an entry in the cash book; when it is on credit the entry is made in the journal and *not* in the purchases day book.

Example of a cash transaction

On January 15 Tom bought a typewriter for £300 plus 15% VAT from L. Wilson & Co., and paid by cheque.

The journal entry will be as follows:

Journal entry to record purchase of an asset for cash

		JOURNAL J6			
Date		Details	Folio No.	Assets	Liabilities
1986 Jan. 15		Office machinery A/c Dr	OM1	£300.00	
✓	✓	VAT	VI	£ 45.00	
✓	✓	Bank	CB9		£345.00
		Being purchase of typewriter machine No. 0659			
		from L. Wilson & Co.			

The entries in the ledger will be as follows:

Ledger entry to record purchase of an asset for cash

LEDGER

DR									CR		
Date	Details	Folio	£	p	Date	Details	Folio	£	p

OFFICE MACHINERY ACCOUNT OM1

Date		Details	Folio	£	p
1986 Jan.	15	Bank	J6	300	00

VAT ACCOUNT V1

Date		Details	Folio	£	p
Jan.	15	Office machinery	J6	45	00

The entry in the payments side of the cash book will be as follows:

Entry in the payments side of the cash book of purchases of an asset for cash

CASH BOOK (Payments side) CB9   CR

Date		Details	Folio	Discount	Input VAT	Net	Cash	Bank
1986 Jan.	15	Office Machinery	J6/V1		45.00	300.00		345.00

Example of a credit transaction

On June 30 Tom bought a van (on credit) for £1,000 plus 15% VAT from XYZ Garages.

The journal entry will be as follows:

Journal entry to record purchase of an asset on credit

JOURNAL J8

Date		Details	Folio No.	Assets	Liabilities
1986 June	30	Motor van A/c	MV1	1,000.00	
		VAT	V1	150.00	
		XYZ Garages	X1		1,150.00
		Being purchase of van Reg. No. B 362 ABX			

The ledger entries will be as follows:

Ledger entries to record purchase of an asset on credit

LEDGER

DR									CR	
Date	Details	Folio	£	p	Date	Details	Folio	£	p	

MOTOR VAN A/c MV1

DR									CR	
1986 June 30	XYZ Garages	J8	1,000	00						

XYZ GARAGES X1

DR									CR	
					1986 June 30	Motor van	J8	1,000	00	
						(Reg. No. B 362 ABX).				
					✓	✓ VAT	J8	150	00	

VAT A/c V2

DR									CR	
1986 June 30	Motor van	J8	150	00						

The rules for journal entries are:

For cash transactions:

- The assets account must be *debited* (receive) the value
- The cash book must be *credited* (payments side) with the value.

For credit transactions (when the asset is to be paid for at future date):
- The assets account must be *debited* (receive) the value
- The supplier must be *credited* with the value of the goods which he has supplied and for which payment is outstanding.

It is always useful to record in the journal the identity of the asset when it is machinery or a vehicle. It is helpful when tracing entries in the files, etc.

Sale of assets (including VAT)

When an asset needs to be sold for whatever reason (it may be worn out, or more modern equipment may be required), it is customary for a firm either to sell it for cash or to 'trade it in' in part payment for its replacement.

Both courses of action entail considering the **book value** recorded in the depreciation account of the asset in the ledger. Bearing in mind that depreciation is only an *estimated* figure there are three possible results:

1) the book value may be absolutely accurate.
2) the book value may exceed the price offered as market value.
3) the book value may be less than the market value.

The book value is accurate

Tom's office machinery account has a typewriter valued at £200 on December 31, 1985. Tom sells it to a local trader for £200 plus 15% VAT (paid by cheque) on January 3, 1986.

The journal entry will be as follows:

Journal entry to record sale of an asset for book value

Date		Details	Folio No.	Assets	Liabilities
1986 Jan.	3	Bank	CB9	£230.00	
✓	✓	Office machinery account	OM1		£200.00
✓	✓	VAT	V3		£30.00
		Being sale of typewriter No.21 to C.Cross			

JOURNAL J12

The entry in the receipts side of Tom's cash book will be as follows:

Entry in receipts side of cash book of sale of an asset for book value

DR		Details	Folio	Discount	Output VAT	Net	Cash	Bank
1986 Jan.	3	Office Machinery A/c	J12		30.00	200.00		230.00

CASH BOOK (Receipts side) CB9

116

The ledger entries will be as follows:

Ledger entry to record sale of an asset for book value

LEDGER

DR											CR
Date	Details	Folio	£	p	Date	Details	Folio	£	p		
					OFFICE MACHINERY A/c OMI						
1985 Dec. 31	Balance	b/d	200	00	1986 Jan. 3	Bank	J12	200	00		
		VAT A/c	V3 (OUTPUT)								
					1986 Jan. 3	Office machinery	J12	30	00		

This means that this machine is now written off in the ledger.

The book value exceeds the price offered as market value

Let us assume that a duplicator with a book value of £250 was sold for £200 plus 15% VAT (paid by cheque) on May 31, 1986. The 'loss' of £50 will be debited to the depreciation account.

The journal entry will be:

Journal entries to record sale of an asset at a loss

JOURNAL J13

Date		Details		Folio No.	Assets	Liabilities
1986 May 31		Bank	Dr	CB10	£230·00	
✓	✓	Depreciation A/c		DA1	£50·00	
✓	✓	Office Machinery A/c		OM1		£250·00
✓	✓	VAT		V1		£30·00
		Being sale of duplicator machine No.631 at				
		£50 less than the book value Folio OM1				

- The asset account must always be *credited* with the book value
- The balance is *debited* to the depreciation account.

117

The entry on the receipts side of the cash book will be as follows:

Entry in receipts side of cash book of sale of an asset at a loss

DR							
CASH BOOK (Receipts side) CB 10							
Date	Details	Folio	Discount	Output VAT	Net	Cash	Bank
1986 May 31	Office machinery A/c			30·00	200·00		230·00

The ledger entries will be as follows:

Ledger entries to record sale of an asset at a loss

LEDGER										
DR										CR
Date	Details	Folio	£	p	Date	Details	Folio	£	p	
		DEPRECIATION A/c	DA1							
1986 May 31	Office machinery	J13	50	00						
		OFFICE MACHINERY A/c OM1								
1986 Jan. 1	Balance	b/d	250	00	1986 May 31	Bank	J13	200	00	
					✓	✓ Depreciation	DA1	50	00	
			£250	00				£250	00	
		VAT A/c V1.								
					1986 May 31	Office machinery	J13	30	00	

The asset account has now been closed. The depreciation will be shown in the profit and loss account when the final accounts are being prepared.

The book value is less than the market value

Tom has a car with a book value of £550 at January 1, 1986. When he sold it on June 1, 1986 £650 plus 15% VAT was realised. The difference of £100 (a gain) will be *credited* to the depreciation account:

The journal entries will be as follows:

Journal entries to record sale of an asset for a gain

Date			Details		Folio No.	Assets	Liabilities
1986 June	1		Bank	Dr	CB6	£747.50	
✓	✓		VAT		V1		£97.50
✓	✓		Motor car A/c		MC1		£550.00
✓	✓		Depreciation A/c		D1		£100.00
			Being sale of car Reg. No. XYA 523 at a profit				

The entry on the receipts side of the cash book will be as follows:

Entry in the receipts side of cash book of sale of an asset for a gain

DR		**CASH BOOK** (Receipts side) CB6						
Date		Details	Folio	Discount	Output VAT	Net	Cash	Bank
1986 June	1	Motor car sale	J14		97.50	650.00		747.50
		Reg. No XYA 523						

The ledger entries will be as shown on the next page:

Ledger entries to record sale of an asset for a gain

LEDGER									
DR									**CR**
Date	Details	Folio	£	p	Date	Details	Folio	£	p
		MOTOR	CAR A/c			MC1			
1986 Jan. 1	Balance	b/d 550		00	1986 June 1	Sale Reg. No. XYA523	J14	550	00
		DEPRECIATION A/c				D1			
					1986 June 1	Motor car	J14	100	00
		VAT	A/c V1						
					1986 June 1	Motor car	J14	97	50

The asset account has been closed in the ledger. The depreciation account's credit will be shown in the profit and loss account.

Correction of errors

Once a figure has been entered in the ledger it must never be erased, overwritten or obliterated. When an error occurs it should be corrected by means of a journal entry and from there posted to the ledger.

Most errors require a double-entry and the account which is to be debited must be entered as the *first* item in the journal.

We will assume that the following errors were found in Tom's books at August 30, 1985, when a trial balance was being prepared. (In order to concentrate on the principle of correction of errors these exercises are exclusive of VAT.)

- *Error 1* A purchase invoice received from D. Davis for £60, dated August 2, has been omitted from the purchases day book.
- *Error 2* A sales day book entry of £350 on August 9 has been debited to T. Thomas instead of R. T. Thomas.
- *Error 3* A new filing cabinet, bought August 19 for £100 (by cheque), has been debited by mistake to the repairs and renewals account.
- *Error 4* Discount of £50 was allowed to T. Ho. This was correctly entered on the receipts side of the cash book on August 21 but it was entered on the credit side of the ledger as £30.

The entries required to correct these errors are shown on the following pages.

Error 1

The error was a complete omission from the purchases day book. The entry should have been shown as:

PURCHASES DAY BOOK PDB1									
Date		Details		Invoice No.	Folio	£	p	£	p
1985 Aug. 21	D. Davis	Goods		33	D1			60	00

Let us say the total purchases for the month were £2,000, and £2,000 was posted to the purchases account, whereas the correct figure is £2,060.

To correct this deficit the following entries will be made, first in the journal.

Entries in journal to correct omission from day book

JOURNAL J3						
Date		Details		Folio No.	Assets	Liabilities
1985 Aug.	30	Purchases A/c		PA1	£60.00	
✓	✓	D. Davis A/c		D1		£60.00
		Being Invoice No. 33 omitted from the purchases day book total.				

The ledger entry will be as follows:

Entry in ledger to correct omission from day book

LEDGER											
DR											**CR**
Date		Details	Folio	£	p	Date		Details	Folio	£	p
				D. DAVIS	D1						
						1985 Aug.	30	Purchases A/c	J3	60	00

LEDGER

DR							CR			
Date	Details	Folio	£	p	Date	Details	Folio	£	p	
		PURCHASES	A/C	PA1						
1985 Aug. 30	Total for month	PDB1	2,000	00						
✓ 21	D. Davis	J3	60	00						

Error 2

This error occurred when posting £350 from the sales day book to the ledger. It was entered as follows:

Incorrect account debited in ledger

LEDGER

DR							CR			
Date	Details	Folio	£	p	Date	Details	Folio	£	p	
		T. THOMAS	A/C	T1						
1985 Aug. 9	Sales	SDB1	350	00						

It should have been entered in R. T. Thomas' account.

To correct this error the following entries should be made, first in the journal.

Entries in journal to correct error in posting entry in ledger

JOURNAL J3

Date	Details	Folio No.	Assets	Liabilities
1985 Aug. 9	R. T. Thomas	T2	£350·00	
✓ ✓	T. Thomas	T1		£350·00
	Being sales invoice No. 270 incorrectly posted.			

The ledger entries will be as follows:

Entries in ledger to correct errors in posting

LEDGER

DR											CR
Date	Details	Folio	£	p	Date	Details	Folio	£	p		
		R.T. THOMAS A/C			T2						
1985 Aug. 9	T. Thomas	J3	350	00							
		T. THOMAS A/C			T1						
1985 Aug. 9	Sales	SDB1	350	00	1985 Aug. 30	R.T. Thomas	J3	350	00		
	(before correction)					(now corrected)					

Error 3

This error was made by posting an asset to the wrong nominal account in the ledger, in this instance the repairs and renewals account instead of the office furniture account.

Posting of asset to wrong account in ledger

LEDGER

DR											CR
Date	Details	Folio	£	p	Date	Details	Folio	£	p		
		REPAIRS +			RENEWALS ACCOUNT R1						
1985 Aug. 19	Bank	CB1	100	00							

To correct this error the following entries will be made, first in the journal.

Entries in journal to correct posting of an asset to wrong account.

JOURNAL J3					
Date	Details	Folio No.	Assets	Liabilities	
1985 Aug. 19	Office furniture A/c	OF1	£100.00		
✓ ✓	Repairs + renewals A/c	R1		£100.00	
	Being invoice No. 275 incorrectly posted.				

The ledger entries will be as follows.

Entries in ledger to correct posting of asset to wrong account

LEDGER										
DR										**CR**
Date	Details	Folio	£	p	Date	Details	Folio	£	p	
		OFFICE FURNITURE			A/C OF1					
1985 Aug. 19	Repairs + renewals	J3	100	00						
		REPAIRS + RENEWALS			A/C R1					
1985 Aug. 19	Bank (before correction)	CB1	100	00	1985 Aug. 30	Office furniture A/c (now corrected)	J3	100	00	

Error 4

Let us say that the original bill was for £2,000. On this the discount allowed was $2\frac{1}{2}\%$ – £50. Therefore this amount was correctly posted in the cash book (see below), but the error arose when it was posted to T. Ho in the ledger as £30:

Correct entry in receipts side of cash book of discount allowed

DR					CASH	BOOK CB3					CR
	RECEIPTS						PAYMENTS				
Date	Details	Folio	Discount Allowed	Cash	Bank	Date	Details	Folio	Discount Received	Cash	Bank
1985 Aug. 21	T. Ho	H1	£50.00		£1,950.00						

Incorrect entry of discount allowed in ledger

LEDGER

DR										CR
Date	Details	Folio	£	p	Date	Details	Folio	£	p	
			T. Ho	H1						
					1985 Aug. 21	Bank	CB3	1,950	00	
					✓ ✓	Discount	CB3	30	00	

To correct this error the following entries will be made, first in the journal.

Entries in journal to correct error in posting discount allowed in ledger

JOURNAL J3

Date	Details	Folio No.	Assets	Liabilities
1985 Aug. 31	Discount allowed A/c	H1	£30.00	
✓ ✓	T. Ho	H1		£50.00
	Being correction of discount allowed.			

The ledger entries will be as follows:

Ledger entries to correct error in posting discount allowed

LEDGER

DR										CR
Date	Details	Folio	£	p	Date	Details	Folio	£	p	
			T. Ho	H1						
1985 Aug. 31	Discount	J3	30	00	1985 Aug. 21	Bank	CB3	1,950	00	
✓ ✓	Balance	c/d	1,950	00	✓ ✓	Discount	CB3	30	00	
			1,980	00				1,980	00	
					Sept. 1	Balance	b/d	1,950	00	
					✓ ✓	Discount	J3	50	00	

Dishonoured (or returned) cheques

A cheque can sometimes be returned to the firm by the bank because the person who issued it does not have enough funds in his or her bank account to cover the amount. The cheque is **dishonoured**.

This means that the debt for which the cheque was issued is still unpaid. The cash book balance and the ledger account will need to be adjusted.

Example

On September 1, 1985, T. Southall owed Tom £50.00. On September 10, a cheque for this amount was paid to Tom by Mr Southall.

Tom recorded the cheque in his cash book, posted the entry to T. Southall's account in the ledger, and banked the cheque on September 13. On September 24 the bank returned the cheque to Tom marked 'RD' (return to drawer – T. Southall).

To make the necessary alterations in the ledger and the cash book a journal entry is needed.

Journal entries to record a returned cheque

Date		Details	Folio No.	Assets	Liabilities
1985 Sept. 24		T. Southall Dr	S1	£50·00	
✓	✓	Bank	CB6		£50·00
		Being dishonoured cheque dated September 10, 1985			

JOURNAL J8 *(heading)*

The ledger entry will be as follows:

Ledger entry to record a returned cheque

LEDGER

Date	Details	Folio	£	p	Date	Details	Folio	£	p
			T. SOUTHALL	S1					
1985 Sept. 1	Sales	SDB1	50	00	1985 Sept. 10	Bank	CB2	50	00
Sept. 24	Bank	J8	50	00					

DR · **CR**

This shows that the £50 is still owing to Tom.

Tom returns the dishonoured cheque to T. Southall with a demand for an immediate payment.

The cash book entries will be as follows:

Cash book entries to record a returned cheque

DR						CASH BOOK CB6					CR
RECEIPTS						PAYMENTS					
Date	Details	Folio	Discount Allowed	Cash	Bank	Date	Details	Folio	Discount Received	Cash	Bank
1985 Sept. 10	T. Southall	S1			£50·00	1985 Sept. 24	T. Southall	J8			£50·00

Folio numbers are very important. They record where each entry has originated:

- The folio numbers have been inserted in the journal after each item has been posted, i.e. S1 is T. Southall's account folio number; CB6 is the relevant cash book folio number.
- In T. Southall's account the debit entry for Sept. 24 of Bank £50 has the journal folio J8 for reference.
- The cash book credit for Sept. 24 of T. Southall £50 also shows that the entry has originated in the journal J8.

Suspense accounts

In Volume 1, Chapter 12, we looked at errors which may not be disclosed when the trial balance is completed. Sometimes the time consumed searching through the books in order to find the differences between the totals of the debits and those of the credits in a trial balance is not profitable to a busy accounts department. A **suspense account** is therefore introduced which records the difference in the balance for the time being, and the errors are discovered at a later date.

Example 1

Tom's trial balance for the year ended July 31, 1985 does not agree. The debit total is £105 greater than the credit total. A suspense account is opened to record this difference.

The result of this entry will mean that the trial balance totals will now agree for July 31, 1985.

Opening of a suspense account in ledger to record difference in trial balance

LEDGER													
DR													**CR**
Date		Details	Folio	£	p	Date		Details	Folio	£	p
			SUSPENSE ACCOUNT S2								
						1985 July	31	Difference in trial balance		105	00

When the book-keeper was taking out the trial balance for the next month (August) it was discovered that an invoice had been entered twice in the debtors' ledger.

The original entry was as follows:

Original entry in debtor's account

LEDGER											
DR											**CR**
Date		Details	Folio	£	p	Date		Details	Folio	£	p
			R. COLES C1								
1985 July	2	Sales	SDB2	105	00						

R. Coles lost the invoice for this transaction whilst moving to new premises, so he requested another copy. This was posted to him on July 26. The sales ledger clerk entered it again in the ledger as follows:

Incorrect second entry in debtor's account

LEDGER											
DR											**CR**
Date		Details	Folio	£	p	Date		Details	Folio	£	p
				R. COLES C1							
1985 July	2	Sales	SDB2	105	00						
July	26	Sales	SDB2	105	00						

Another entry was not made in the sales day book, however, so the sales account remained correct.

Returning to the trial balance we now see that the debit side was £105 too much. We must correct this error by a journal entry so that we can amend R. Coles' account and close the suspense account.

The journal entry will be:

Journal entries to correct error in ledger and close suspense account

JOURNAL J5						
Date		Details		Folio No.	Assets	Liabilities
1985 Aug.	21	Suspense A/c		S2	105·00	
		R. Coles A/c		C1		105·00
		Being error in posting R. Cole's account on July 2.				

The ledger entry for R. Coles' account will be as follows:

Ledger entries to correct debtor's account and close suspense account

LEDGER										
DR										**CR**
Date	Details	Folio	£	p	Date	Details	Folio	£	p	
			R.COLES C1							
1985 July	2	Sales	SDB2	105	00	1985 Aug. 31	Suspense A/c	J5	105	00
July	26	Sales	SDB2	105	00	✓ ✓	Balance	c/d	105	00
				210	00				210	00
Sept.	1	Balance	b/d	105	00					

129

The ledger entry for the suspense account will be as follows:

Entry in suspense account to correct difference in trial balance

LEDGER

DR									**CR**
Date	Details	Folio	£	p	Date	Details	Folio	£	p
		SUSPENSE		A/C		S2			
1985 Aug. 31	R. Coles	J5	105	00	1986 July 31	Difference in trial balance		105	00

Example 2

On December 31 R. Palin's trial balance for the end of the year failed to agree. The credit balance total was £233 less than the debit balance. A suspense account was opened as follows:

Opening of a suspense account to record difference in trial balance

LEDGER

DR									**CR**
Date	Details	Folio	£	p	Date	Details	Folio	£	p
		SUSPENSE		ACCOUNT		S1			
					1985 Dec. 31	Difference in trial balance		233	00

The following errors were found in January:

1) Sales to T. Wren for £28 had been posted to the debit of S. Wrench.
2) Cash discount of £30 had been allowed to P. Mancini and had been correctly credited to his account but no entry had been made in the discount allowed account.
3) A typewriter sold for £280 had been credited to the sales account.
4) The addition of the sales account had been undercast by £95.
5) A balance of £168 for the rent owing had been omitted from the ledger.

The journal entries needed to correct these errors will be as follows.

Entries in journal to correct errors in book-keeping

			JOURNAL J6			
	Date		Details	Folio No.	Assets	Liabilities
1)	1986 Dec. 31 ✓	31 ✓	T. Wren Dr S. Wrench Being misposting of sales to the ledger.	W1 W2	£28·00	£28·00
2)	✓ ✓	✓ ✓	Discount allowed Dr Suspense account Being total of discount allowed omitted from the trial balance.	DA1 S1	£30·00	£30·00
3)	✓ ✓	✓ ✓	Sales A/c Dr Office machines A/c Being asset incorrectly posted.	SA1 OM1	£280·00	£280·00
4)	✓ ✓	✓ ✓	Suspense A/c Dr Sales A/c Being incorrect total c/f for sales A/c	S1 SA1	£95·00	£95·00
5)	1985 Dec. 31 ✓	31 ✓	Suspense A/c Dr Rent A/c Being balance omitted from the ledger and the trial balance.	S1 R1	£168·00	£168·00

The suspense account will now look like this.

Ledger entries to close the suspense account

DR											CR
LEDGER											
Date		Details	Folio	£	p	Date	Details	Folio	£	p	
			SUSPENSE		ACCOUNT S1						
1986 Jan. 31		Sales A/c	J6	95	00	1985 Dec. 31	Difference in		233	00	
✓	✓	Rent A/c	J6	168	00		trial balance				
						✓	✓ Discount allowed	J6	30	00	
				£263	00				£263	00	

These entries have been made in the journal for the following reasons.

1) These two entries are both in the debtors' ledger accounts and are simply transferred (see ledger entries below.) The trial balance is not affected.

2) This is known as an **omission error.** The discount allowed account is short by £30.00. It is 'paired' with the suspense account because it was omitted in the ledger and the trial balance (credit totals).

3) This is known as an **error of principle**. The sale of an asset has been included in the sale of goods. It does *not* affect the totals of the trial balance.

4) This is known as an **original error**. The total for the sales account is incorrect and forms part of the suspense account because it affects the trial balance.

5) The balance on the credit side of the rent account has been omitted. The credit balance in the trial balance is undercast by £233. Hence it is part of the suspense account.

The ledger entries needed will be as follows.

Ledger entries to correct errors in book-keeping

LEDGER											
DR											**CR**
Date		Details	Folio	£	p	Date		Details	Folio	£	p
			T. WREN		W1						
1985 Dec.	31	S.Wrench	J6	28	00						
			S.WRENCH		W2						
						1985 Dec.	31	T.Wren	J6	28	00
			DISCOUNT ALLOWED	ACCOUNT	DA1						
1985 Dec.	31	Suspense A/c	J6	30	00						
			OFFICE MACHINERY	ACCOUNT	OM1						
						1985 Dec.	31	Sales	J6	280	00
			SALES	ACCOUNT	SA1						
1985 Dec.	31	Office machinery A/c	OM1	280	00	1985 Dec.	31	Total sales	J6	95	00
			RENT	ACCOUNT	R1						
						1985 Dec.	31	Suspense A/c	S1	168	00

Chapter 9 Exercises

Purchase of assets

1 *M. Milton bought the following assets for his business and paid by cheque on May 1, 1986.*

Plant and machinery	£14,000
Motor vans	£2,500
Stock	£1,000
Furniture and refrigerated counters	£500

The above purchases are subject to 15% VAT.

- *Make the journal entries for these assets.*

- *Open the necessary accounts.*

2 *On January 16, 1986, the Dunhelm Camping Supply Co. supplied the Gatehouse Camping Club with the following equipment on credit:*

Tents	£400
Windbreaks	£200
Tools	£150
Ground-sheets	£50

Allow for VAT at 15%

- *Make the journal entries.*

- *Post the entries to the ledger.*

3 *On March 1, 1985 the Hillsview Disco Club bought new recording equipment for the club, from the Farndale Company. The treasurer paid a cheque for £71.19 which included 15% VAT.*

- *Make the journal entries for the assets.*

- *Open the necessary accounts.*

4 *On June 30, 1986 Alma Rushton bought on credit a display unit Model No. X532 for the dress shop from Parkside Shopfitters Limited. It cost £76.37 including 15% VAT.*

- *Make the journal entries for the asset.*

- *Open the necessary accounts.*

5 On November 17, 1985 Lyle Snair, a builder, purchased on credit a sanding machine Model 2Ax from Economy Builders Suppliers. The invoice showed a cost of £965.06 plus 15% VAT.

- Make the journal entries.
- Open the necessary accounts.

6 On December 17, 1985 Lyle Snair bought a truck, Reg. No. A392 BDC, from Herrington Trucks Limited. The cost was £5,000 plus VAT at 15%. A trade in price of £1,000 was allowed for his old truck, Reg. No. NTN 205V, which had a book value of £1,200. Lyle Snair paid by cheque £4,600.

- Make the journal entries for the new asset. Show the allowance for the old vehicle.
- Open the necessary accounts.
- Balance the vehicle account at December 31, 1985.

Sale of assets

1 On October 16, 1985, Tom Robinson sold a printing machine (No. 4360) for £250, which was exactly the amount shown as its scrap value in the ledger. Make the journal entry for this sale and show the closed ledger account. Make the appropriate entry in the cash book. The sale was subject to 15% VAT.

2 On October 26, 1985, Tom Robinson sold, on credit, a paper shredding machine (No. 502) for £350 to L. Kamarinsky. Its book value was £450.

Allow 15% VAT.

- Make the journal entry for this transaction and close the ledger account.
- Show the entries made in the depreciation account.
- Open an account for this credit transaction.

3 On March 31, 1986, Tom Robinson sold a motor-van for £385 plus 15% VAT for which he received a cheque for £257.75, which included the VAT. The balance was to be paid within the month. The buyer was C. Krotke. The book value of the van was £200.
Allow 15% VAT.

Show the entries for this transaction in:

- the journal
- the cash book
- the motor van and depreciation accounts
- C. Krotke's ledger account.

4 On March 30, 1986 the Heavy Plant & Machinery Co. sold a mechanical digger, model No. 631 with a book value of £10,000, for £8,000 plus 15% VAT to Pillar Land Reclaim Company, who settled their account by cheque.

- Make the journal entry for this transaction and close the ledger account.

- Show the entries made in the depreciation account, VAT account and the cash book.

5 On December 31, 1985 Kevin Foster, a dairyman, sold on credit a milking machine, model No. 23 with a book value of £950, for £1,000 plus 15% VAT to N. Veal.

- Make the journal entry for this transaction and the ledger accounts.

6 On August 15, 1985 Brian Parker, a jeweller, sold a safe with a book value of £3,500 for £3,500 plus 15% VAT. The buyer was Tessa Kay. She paid £525 and the balance was to be paid within the month.

- Make the journal entries for this transaction and the appropriate ledger accounts.

Correction of errors

1 Show the journal entries for the following errors. Date the journal December 31, 1985.

- Goods purchased from A. Thompson for £50.00 has been posted in the ledger as T. Thomson £50.00
- A duplicator bought on credit from G. Grade has been posted to the purchases account in the ledger, the amount being £300.
- Depreciation of £100 on a typewriter has been credited to fixtures and fittings account.
- When paying R. Raman for goods supplied, T. Robinson deducted discount of £3. R. Raman has disallowed this discount because the account was not paid within the allotted time.
- A sale of goods on credit to L. Lasky amounting to £250 has been entered in the sales day book as £230 and has been posted to the ledger as £230.

Suspense accounts

1 *On December 31, 1985, P. McSwain extracted a trial balance. The debit side of the trial balance totalled £21,130, and the credit side £20,867. A suspense account was opened for the difference. During the month of January he discovered the following errors which accounted for the difference.*

- *The total of the purchases day book for the month of December was £3,479, but had been posted to the purchases account as £3,749.*
- *The discount received account in the cash book had been wrongly totalled and posted to the discount received account as £67 instead of £69.*
- *A cheque for £176 paid for rent had been posted to the rent account as £167.*
- *A credit note sent to A. Battle for £16.50 had been entered into the sales returns book and posted to the sales returns account as £10.80.*

Make the journal entries to correct these errors and show the suspense account after the corrections have been made.

2 *P. Klein's trial balance for May 31, 1986 did not balance, and a suspense account was opened in which the difference was entered. The amount of the difference was £430 on the credit side. A detailed checking of the books in June disclosed the following errors.*

- *The purchases returns for May, £100, was posted to the debit side of the purchases account.*
- *The sales day book total for May was £10 short.*
- *Discount received of £120 was posted to the debit side of the account.*
- *A sale of goods to A. Baratra for £10 was correctly recorded in the sales day book but was posted to A. Baratra's account as £5.*
- *A bill for £5 for stationery paid by cash in the cash book was not posted to the stationery account.*

Make the journal entries to correct the above errors, and show the suspense account after the corrections have been made.

Answers are given in the *Worked Solutions.*

10 Simple Ledger Control Accounts

The ledger as described in Chapter 6 of Volume 1 contains the three sections personal, impersonal and nominal accounts. (Note that since impersonal accounts refer to such things as furniture, tools, land, etc. they are often called real or property accounts.) In the early days of book-keeping one bound ledger was sufficient to contain all three sections. When the ledger became full the various accounts were transferred to a new book, and new headings were raised for each account.

With the growth of modern business there is an ever increasing number of accounts comprising assets and liabilities, expenses and gains, debtors and creditors to be recorded. Of these, debtors and creditors accounts make up the largest proportion, and for these it is more practical to use several loose-leaf binders in place of the single old-fashioned bound ledger. The binders are normally arranged alphabetically – one for all the debtors, for example, A–D, E–G, and so on; similarly for all the creditors. The loose-leaf binders allow for extra sheets to be slotted in when required and others to be removed when no longer current.

This method of using several ledgers for debtors and creditors accounts makes it easy for more than one clerk to be responsible for posting the entries and balancing the accounts when taking out a trial balance. If the trial balance does not agree there could be a very tedious and time-consuming number of additions and entries to be checked.

A **control account** is a very useful means of reducing the number of entries to be checked in both the debtors and creditors accounts. Also known as a total account, a control account is one which contains the total figures – the sum of the individual accounts which apply to the debtors and creditors accounts. It is a memorandum for recording the various totals from the subsidiary books and is generally kept at the back of the relevant ledger. In the event of a trial balance not agreeing the control account helps to indicate which of the subsidiary books contains an error.

Control account for the debtors ledger

This account contains:

- the opening debit and credit balances from the ledger brought down from the previous month;
- total sales for the month (posted from the sales day book);
- total cash received (net of output VAT) posted from the cash book;

- total discount allowed (net of output VAT) posted from the cash book;
- total returns inward (net of output VAT) from the returns inward book;
- total output VAT;
- journal entries applicable to the debtors, such as bad debts;
- total credit balances at the end of the month (the date of the control account).

For the purposes of a control account the subsidiary books will be ruled with analysis columns (similar to those shown in departmental accounts later in Chapter 14).

SALES DAY BOOK SDB1 DEBTORS A–D											
Date	Details	Invoice	Folio	Dept. A		Dept. B		Total			
				Net	Output VAT	Net	Output VAT	Net A	Net B	Output VAT A	B

Total sales for the month are posted to the sales account (SA1) in the ledger.

The same applies to the returns inward book and the cash book.

We will now prepare the sales ledger control account entering the following totals for the month of January 1986 taken from the subsidiary books for the Debtors A–D. (We will omit total output VAT.)

1986
Jan. 1   Opening sales ledger debit balance b/d
from December1985   £10,966

Opening sales ledger credit balance b/d
from December 1985   £900

Jan. 31   Total sales day book (net of
output VAT)   £41,120
Cash from debtors (net of output VAT)   £32,150
Discount allowed   £1,620
Returns inward (net of output VAT)   £820
Bad debt written off in the journal   £180
Closing sales ledger credit balances   £75

It will be noted that there are opening and closing balances on both sides. This is because there will often be money owing to the debtors by the firm (perhaps an invoice has been overcharged or a credit note may be outstanding for goods returned inward, etc.). Some of the debtors' accounts are therefore in credit.

SALES LEDGER CONTROL ACCOUNT A–D

DR				CR			
Date	Details	Folio	£ p	Date	Details	Folio	£ p
1986				1986			
Jan. 1	Balances	b/d	10,966.00	Jan. 1	Balance	b/d	900.00
Jan. 31	Sales	SDB1	41,120.00	Jan. 31	Cash	CB1	32,150.00
✓	Balance	c/d	75.00	✓	Disc. allowed	CB1	1,620.00
				✓	Rtns inw.	RIB1	820.00
				✓	Bad debts	J1	180.00
				✓	Balance	c/d	16,491.00
			£52,161.00				£52,161.00
Feb. 1	Balance	b/d	16,491.00	Feb. 1	Balance	b/d	75.00

Control account for the creditors ledger

This account contains:

- the opening credit and debit balances from the ledger brought down from the previous month;
- the total purchases (net of input VAT) from the purchases day book;
- the total payments to creditors (net of input VAT) from the cash book;
- the total discount received;
- returns outward (net of input VAT) from the returns outward book;
- total input VAT;
- the journal entries which apply to the creditors ledger;
- the total debit balances at the end of the month (the date of the control account).

We will now prepare the purchases ledger control account, omitting total input VAT.

1986		
Jan. 1	Opening debit balance from purchases ledger b/d from December 1985	£200
	Opening credit balance from purchases ledger b/d from December 1985	£5,483
Jan. 31	Total purchases for month (posted from purchases day book) (net of input VAT)	£52,860
	Cash paid to creditors (net of input VAT)	£53,796
	Discount received	£460
	Returns outward (net of input VAT)	£632
	Closing purchases ledger balances	£275

PURCHASE LEDGER CONTROL ACCOUNTS A–D

DR   **CR**

Date	Details	Folio	£ p	Date	Details	Folio	£ p
1986				1986			
Jan. 1	Opening balance	b/d	200.00	Jan. 1	Balances	b/d	5,483.00
Jan. 31	Cash	CB1	53,796.00	Jan. 31	Purchases	PDB1	52,860.00
✓	Disc. rcd.	CB1	460.00	✓	Balances	c/d	275.00
✓	Rtns out.	ROB1	632.00				
✓	Balance	c/d	3,530.00				
			£58,618.00				£58,618.00
Feb. 1	Balance	b/d	275.00	Feb. 1	Balance	b/d	3,530.00

There are balances on both sides because the firm is owed money by the supplier (creditor). Possibly goods were returned as being unsatisfactory (returns outward) and a credit note is outstanding, or again the supplier may have overcharged on an invoice. The supplier is a debtor to the firm.

Contra entries in control accounts

These are entries which occur when a supplier also buys goods from his/her customer. For example, D. Clarke who manufactures inks, dyes, etc. supplies T. Robinson with goods valued at £100. T. Robinson sells printed labels and stationery to D. Clarke for £65.

There are two accounts in D. Clarke's ledger as follows:

1) *Debtors ledger*

LEDGER

DR   **CR**

Date	Details	Folio	£ p	Date	Details	Folio	£ p
			T. ROBINSON R1				
1986				1986			
Jan. 6	Sales	SDB1	100.00				

141

2) *Creditors ledger*

LEDGER

DR							CR
Date	Details	Folio	£ p	Date	Details	Folio	£ p
			T. ROBINSON R2				
1986							
				Jan. 10	Purchases	PDB1	65.00

From these accounts we see that T. Robinson only owes D. Clarke £35. To show this as a 'contra' entry in the ledger we must first enter it in the journal.

JOURNAL J6

DR					CR
Date	Details	Folio	Assets		Liabilities
1986					
Jan. 31	T. Robinson (creditors ledger) Dr	R1	£65.00		
✓	T. Robinson (debtors ledger)	R2			£65.00
	Being 'contra' entry to balance creditors ledger				

These journal entries are now posted to D. Clarke's accounts:

1) *Debtors ledger*

DEBTORS LEDGER

DR							CR
Date	Details	Folio	£ p	Date	Details	Folio	£ p
			T. Robinson R1				
1986				1986			
Jan. 6	Sales	SDB1	100.00	Jan. 31	Contra	J6	65.00
				✓	Purchase ledger		35.00
					Balance c/d		
			100.00				100.00
Feb. 1	Balance c/d		35.00				

2) *Creditors ledger*

CREDITORS LEDGER

DR							CR
Date	Details	Folio	£ p	Date	Details	Folio	£ p
			T. Robinson R2				
1986				1986			
Jan. 31	Contra	J6	65.00	Jan. 10	Purchases	PDB1	65.00
	Sales ledger						

We will show how the above 'contra' entry now appears in D. Clarke's sales ledger control account and the purchases ledger control account. (All the entries are net of VAT.)

1986
Jan. 1	Opening debit balance from the sales ledger	£7,206
Jan. 31	Opening credit balance from the sales ledger	£64
	Opening debit balance from the purchases ledger	£4,569
	Opening credit balance from the purchases ledger	£54
	Cash received from debtors	£8,612
	Sales to debtors	£9,200
	Cash paid to creditors	£3,520
	Purchases for the month	£12,500
	Returns outwards	£216
	Returns inwards	£310
	Carriage outwards	£25
	'Contra' entry from purchases ledger to sales ledger (credit)	£65
	Closing credit balance from the sales ledger	£100
	Closing debit balance from the purchases ledger	£300

SALES LEDGER CONTROL ACCOUNT

DR   **CR**

Date	Details	Folio	£ p	Date	Details	Folio	£ p
1986				1986			
Jan. 1	Balance	b/d	7,206.00	Jan. 1	Balance	b/d	64.00
Jan. 31	Sales	SDB1	9,200.00	Jan. 31	Cash	CB1	8,612.00
✓	Carriage	C1	25.00	✓	Rtns in	RIB1	310.00
✓	Contra	J6	65.00	✓	Balance	c/d	7,610.00
✓	Balance	c/d	100.00				
			£16,596.00				£16,596.00
Feb. 1	Balance	b/d	7,610.00	Feb. 1	Balance	b/d	100.00

PURCHASES LEDGER CONTROL ACCOUNT

DR   **CR**

Date	Details	Folio	£ p	Date	Details	Folio	£ p
1986				1986			
Jan. 1	Balance	b/d	4,569.00	Jan. 1	Balance	b/d	54.00
Jan. 31	Cash	CB1	3,520.00	Jan. 31	Purchases	PDB1	12,500.00
✓	Rtns out	ROB1	216.00	✓	Contra	J6	65.00
✓	Balance	c/d	4,614.00	✓	Balance	c/d	300.00
			£12,919.00				£12,919.00
Feb. 1	Balance	b/d	300.00	Feb. 1	Balance	b/d	4,614.00

Use of control accounts

We said earlier in the chapter that the control account helps to reduce the items to be checked when a trial balance is being prepared. The following is an example of reconciling the sales control account with the list of debtors balance when it is discovered that they do not agree.

It was discovered at the end of January that D. Clarke's trial balance did not balance. The total of the list of debit balances in the sales ledgers A–D showed a total of £6,037. The sales control account (shown on page 144) has a balance brought down to February 1 of £7,610.

The first step was to check the entries in the subsidiary books A–D. This resulted in the following errors being discovered:

- an invoice for £176 to T. Dobbins in the sales day book had been omitted from the ledger;
- the total of the sales day book is £265 short;
- the returns inward book is £200 short;
- a 'contra' entry in the purchases ledger of £532 has been omitted from the control account;
- in the sales ledger an entry of £400 discount allowed has been omitted.

This is how we reconcile the sales ledger list of balances with the sales ledger control account:

**								

SALES LEDGER CONTROL ACCOUNT

DR								CR
Date	Details	Folio	£ p	Date	Details	Folio	£ p
1986 Feb. 1	Original balance	b/d	7,610.00	Jan. 31	Sales day book	SDB1	265.00
				✓	Rtns inw. book	RIB1	200.00
				✓	Contra	J1	532.00
				✓	Balance	c/d	6,613.00
			£7,610.00				£7,610.00
Feb. 1	Balance	b/d	6,613.00				

List of Debtors' Balances – Ledger A–D

	£
Original total	6,037
Add Invoice T. Dobbins, December 31, 1986	176
Discount allowed	400
	£6,613

Chapter 10 Exercises

1 *Mrs Chopra started business on July 1, 1986. Construct control accounts for the following transactions for the month of July 1986.*

Total goods purchased on credit from suppliers	£15,104
Goods returned to suppliers	£628
Cheques paid to suppliers	£9,723
Total goods sold on credit	£45,312
Customers' returned goods value	£205
Cash and cheques received from customers	£38,524
Allowed discount to customers	£963
Received discount from suppliers	£1,200

2 *From the following balances for the month of December, 1985 prepare L. Kamarski's purchases ledger control account and the sales ledger control account for the month.*

Balances:	Sales ledger (debit)	£3,489
	Sales ledger (credit)	£37
	Purchases ledger (debit)	£50
	Purchases ledger (credit)	£8,223
Total credit sales		£30,840
Cash received from debtors		£24,070
Cash paid to creditors		£36,950
Total purchases		£39,640
Discount received		£1,850
Discount allowed		£750
Purchases returns		£183
Sales returns		£920
Bad debts written-off		£300
Credit balances in the purchases ledger 'contra' to the sales ledger		£240
Closing purchase ledger credit balance		£65
Closing sales ledger debit balance		£125

3 *P. Stephanou keeps a separate sales ledger and purchases ledger. You are required to draw up the control account for both ledgers for the month of January 1986.*

Jan. 1	Sales ledger:	Debit balance	£40,809.00
		Credit balance	£69.00
	Purchases ledger:	Credit balance	£8,919.75
		Debit balance	£36.00
	Total sales		£140,324.00

Total purchases	£30,000.00
Total cash received from debtors	£72,920.00
Payments to creditors	£8,440.00
Returns inward	£670.00
Returns outward	£235.00
Bad debts (written off)	£100.00
Sales ledger 'contra' to purchases ledger	£92.00
Carriage outward	£108.00

4 *The trial balance for the month of August 1985 did not agree. The debit balances of the sales ledger totalled £18,418. The sales ledger control account totalled £19,449. The following errors were discovered:*

- *the sales day book total was £500 in excess;*
- *an invoice for £75 was not posted in the sales ledger;*
- *a bad debt for £24 written off in the ledger had not been recorded in the journal;*
- *a 'contra' purchases ledger control account entry was not recorded in the sales ledger control account for £127;*
- *a credit note for £15 was not entered in the returns inward book;*
- *error in the total of the list of balances extracted from the sales ledger £200;*
- *discount received £90 was not posted to the sales ledger.*

Show the adjustments to reconcile the sales control account with the ledger balances.

5 *The trial balance did not agree. The credit balances total was £9,294. The purchases control account showed a net balance of £8,890.*

The following errors were found:

- *a cheque paid to T. Snowdon (a creditor) for £84 was returned as dishonoured; the book-keeper credited Snowdon's account in the ledger but no entry was made in the journal to debit the cash book;*
- *the opening balance in the purchases control account was shown as £8,890, the correct figure from the previous month's records being £8,990;*
- *£10 discount received was disallowed by a supplier;*
- *discount received of £80 was not posted to the supplier's account in the ledger;*
- *a contra sales entry for £140 was not posted in the ledger to clear an account;*
- *an invoice for £10 was also not posted in the ledger.*

Show the adjustments to reconcile the purchases control account with the ledger balances.

Answers are given in the *Worked Solutions.*

11 Simple Partnership Accounts I

Throughout Volume 1, and for most of this book, we have dealt with all the aspects of book-keeping up to final accounts by following the fortunes of one man's business, that of the printer Tom Robinson.

Sole traders

Tom is a **sole trader**, that is a person who is solely responsible for the whole of the business. This means he provides all the capital and is responsible for all the liabilities.

Although in Tom's case it is only a small firm, it is quite possible that a sole trader could be a very large firm indeed, provided the owner had sufficient capital to carry on an extensive business (for example a building contractor).

However, the danger for many small businesses, such as Tom's, is that in the event of a failure the sole trader could lose everything. To meet his debts all his private possessions (his house, his car, etc.), as well as the assets of his business, would have to be sold, and he could be ruined.

Partnerships

One way of safeguarding himself, and of putting his business on a sound footing, would be for Tom to take a **partner**. He could go into partnership with another sole trader (in this case a fellow printer) for their mutual benefit.

A partnership is the joining together of the business of two or more persons in order to increase their capital and to extend their business. A partnership will be legally binding by an agreement called the **partnership deed**.

The partnership deed

This is a legally binding agreement which must be in writing. Below is an example of some of the requirements:

- the amount of capital each partner will provide;
- the date upon which the partnership will start;
- the methods of sharing profits and losses;

- the names of the parties by which the firm will be known;
- the amount of salary (if any) that will be paid to the partners;
- the amount of drawings which will be allowed for the partners in anticipation of a profit being made;
- whether interest will be given on the capital invested;
- whether interest will be charged on drawings;
- anyone who enters into a partnership becomes jointly liable for all the debts and contracts made by the firm from the time he or she enters into the partnership. If a partner dies claims can be made from the estate for his/her share of any debts which are outstanding at the date of his/her death.

A partner who retires from the firm is still liable for partnership debts incurred up to and including the time of his/her retirement.

Tom decided to offer a partnership to Mr W. Wainwright (another printer). They agreed that the requirements given would form the basis of their partnership deed.

Their partnership deed is shown below, and the balance sheets at the close of their separate businesses are shown on page 150.

PARTNERSHIP DEED

1) Capital provided:	T. Robinson £7,306 W. Wainwright £4,530
2) Share of profits and losses:	2/3 Robinson 1/3 Wainwright
3) Date the partnership will start:	Sept. 1, 1986
4) Names of the parties: **Title of the Business:** **Address:**	T. Robinson W. Wainwright Robinson & Wainwright — Printers 3 High Street, Hull
5) Salary:	£100 per annum to be paid to W. Wainwright
6) Drawings:	£100 T. Robinson; £50 W. Wainwright per annum
7) Interest on capital:	4 per cent on £7,306 to T. Robinson

Tom's and W. Wainwright's balance sheets at the close of their separate businesses

T. ROBINSON

BALANCE SHEET

As at August 31, 1986

LIABILITIES	£	£	ASSETS	£	£
Capital	7,056		Fixed assets		
Add Net profit	350		Machinery	1,670	
			Vans	1,200	2,870
	7,406				
Less Drawings	100	7,306			
			Current assets		
			Stock	2,146	
			Debtors	1,950	
Current liabilities			Cash at bank	1,000	
Creditors		900	Cash in hand	240	5,336
		£8,206			£8,206

W. WAINWRIGHT

BALANCE SHEET

as at August 31, 1986

LIABILITIES	£	£	ASSETS	£	£
Capital	4,480		Fixed assets		
Add Net profit	250		Machinery		1,250
	4,730				
Less Drawings	200	4,530	Current assets		
			Stock	1,675	
			Debtors	1,225	
Current liabilities			Cash at bank	970	
Creditors		690	Cash in hand	100	3,970
		£5,220			£5,220

The accounts of the new partnership

The opening journal

The first entry in the journal showing the combined assets of Robinson & Wainwright reads as follows.

Opening entry of the journal of the new partnership

JOURNAL J1

Machinery	2,920	
Vans	1,200	
Stock	3,821	
Debtors	3,175	
Cash at bank	1,970	
Cash in hand	340	
Creditors		1,590
Capital		
T. Robinson		7,306
W. Wainwright		4,530
	13,426	13,426

Being Assets and Liabilities of T. Robinson and W. Wainwright at 1st September 1986.

The ledger accounts

These are recorded in the same way as the ledger accounts of a sole trader, but each partner also has a separate account for each of the following:

- a **capital account** where the original amount invested is shown throughout the duration of the partnership (this figure is also shown in the balance sheet);

The capital accounts of the new partners

LEDGER

DR									**CR**
Date	Details	Folio	£	p	Date	Details	Folio	£	p

T. ROBINSON CA1

Date	Details	Folio	£	p	Date	Details	Folio	£	p
					1985				
					Sept 1	Balance	J1	7,306	00

W. WAINWRIGHT CA

Date	Details	Folio	£	p	Date	Details	Folio	£	p
					1985				
					Sept 1	Balance	J1	4,530	00

- a **current account** which records the salaries, interest on capital, drawings and the share of the profit (or loss).

The current accounts of the new partners

DR											**CR**
Date		Details	Folio	£	p	Date		Details	Folio	£	p
				T. ROBINSON							
				CURRENT ACCOUNT							
1985 Aug.	31	Drawings	CBI	100	00	1985 Aug.	31	Interest on capital		292	00
v	v	Balance	c/a	997	00	v	v	Share of profit		805	00
				£1,097	00					£1,097	00
						Sept.	1	Balance	b/a	997	00
				W. WAINWRIGHT							
				CURRENT ACCOUNT							
1985 Aug.	31	Drawings	CBI	50	00	1985 Aug.	31	Salary	CBI	100	00
v	v	Balance	c/a	453	00	v	v	Share of profit		403	00
				£503	00					£503	00
						Sept.	1	Balance	b/a	453	00

The figures involved in both the capital and current accounts, are also to be seen in the **appropriation account** which is explained further on the next page.

The final accounts

The methods of preparing the trading account and the profit and loss account are the same as those shown in Chapters 1 and 2 of this book. In the profit and loss account, however, there is an additional section called the appropriation account.

The balance sheet too is prepared in the same way as that of a sole trader (see Chapter 3), but the liabilities side has to show the balances of the capital and current accounts. This is dealt with further on page 154.

The appropriation account

The difference between the profit and loss account of a sole trader and that of a partnership is shown in the treatment of the net profit (or net loss).

In a sole trader's account the profit belongs to him or her and as such is added to his or her capital account in the balance sheet (or, in the case of a loss, is deducted).

In a partnership, however, the profit that is left after allowing for salaries and interest on capital (see below) must be divided between the partners according to the partnership agreement. This sharing is shown as a section added to the profit and loss account called the appropriation account.

According to their partnership agreement shown on page 150, in Robinson & Wainwright's accounts the sharing would be $\frac{2}{3}$ Robinson and $\frac{1}{3}$ Wainwright.

Let us assume that their profit and loss account has been prepared with a net profit for the year of £1,600. The appropriation account for the partnership will look like this:

The appropriation account for the new partnership

ROBINSON & WAINWRIGHT

APPROPRIATION ACCOUNT

	£		£
Salary		Net profit b/d from	
W. Wainwright	100	profit and loss account	1,600
Interest on capital			
T. Robinson			
4% on £7,306	292		
Balance being share of profit			
T. Robinson 2/3	805		
W. Wainwright 1/3	403		
	£1,600		£1,600

You will notice that we have ignored the pennies. Accountants always round off the figures to the nearest pound.

Interest obtained on capital

This is an interest charged against profits. Each partner receives interest on the total capital that he has invested in the partnership.

153

This means that if one partner invests more capital than the other then he will receive compensation for the difference in capital invested.

If you look at the partnership deed of Robinson & Wainwright on page 150 you will see that only Robinson receives interest on his capital. Wainwright receives no interest but does have a salary.

The balance sheet

The balance sheet of a partnership on the assets side is prepared in the same way as that of a sole trader. The difference is on the liabilities side where both the capital accounts and the balances of the current accounts are shown, as demonstrated in the following extract from the balance sheet of Robinson & Wainwright.

Extract from the balance sheet of the new partnership

ROBINSON & WAINWRIGHT — PRINTERS

BALANCE SHEET

as at August 31, 1986

LIABILITIES	£	£	ASSETS
Capital accounts			
T. Robinson	7,306		
W. Wainwright	4,530	11,836	
Current accounts			
T. Robinson	997		
W. Wainwright	453	1,450	
Current liabilities			

There is an alternative method of presenting the current accounts in the balance sheet. This will be covered in the next chapter – see page 159.

The Partnership Act 1890

As we have seen, Tom Robinson and W. Wainwright were prudent and entered into a deed of partnership which was legally binding.

However, there are cases where partners neglect to do this. The **Partnership Act** is an Act of Parliament which was introduced in 1890 to safeguard businesses that are *not* controlled by a legally binding partnership deed as between Robinson and Wainwright. In the event of any dispute arising in the business affairs of such a partnership, the Partnership Act 1890 applies.

The sharing of profits and losses is often a cause of conflict between partners in the event of the failure of the business. The Partnership Act 1890 states:

- capital must be equally invested by the partners;
- profits or losses must be shared equally;
- no partner is entitled to a salary for his or her part in the business activities;
- interest is not payable on the partners' capital;
- if a partner lends money to the firm over and above his or her capital he or she shall be entitled to interest of 5% per annum.

Exercises on simple partnership accounts are to be found on pages 167–70, at the end of the following chapter which covers further aspects of the same subject.

12 Simple Partnership Accounts II

In the previous chapter we looked at the partnership deed and accounts of a particular partnership, Robinson & Wainwright. As has been mentioned this is a relatively small firm and does not involve all the items that could arise in a partnership. We will now consider further items which could be contained in more complicated partnership deeds.

Interest charged on drawings

In a partnership the capital is fixed by the amount shown in the partnership deed. As the profit will not be known until the end of the year, unrestricted drawings by the partners could reduce the original capital, leaving a debit balance on the current account. The partner would then be in debt to the firm.

To avoid this happening a partnership deed may include a percentage charge on the drawings. The interest will then be added (credited) to the net profit in the appropriation account and the partner's current account will be charged (debited) with the amount.

As a simple example, assume in a partnership where the net profit is £1,000 one partner draws £500 per annum and the partnership deed allows interest to be charged at 4% per annum, that is £20.

The entry in the appropriation acount will be as follows:

Extract from appropriation account showing interest charged on drawings

	APPROPRIATION ACCOUNT	
		£
	Net profit	1,000
	Interest on drawings 4%	20

The entry in the partner's current account will be as follows.

Entry in partner's current account to record interest charged on drawings

LEDGER										
DR										**CR**
Date	Details	Folio	£	p	Date	Details	Folio	£	p
			CURRENT		ACCOUNT	CA1			
	Drawings	DA1	500	00					
	Interest on	I1	20	00					
	drawings								

Drawings in kind

These are drawings in goods which a partner takes for his private use. They have been bought by the firm and are therefore at cost price. The two accounts involved in this transaction are:

- the purchases account
- the partner's current account.

For example, say T. Patel, a partner in the firm of Patel & Singh, takes £50 worth of goods from stock for his personal use (not for re-sale by the firm) on December 31, 1985.

The ledger entries will be as follows:

Ledger entries to record drawings in kind

LEDGER										
DR										**CR**
Date	Details	Folio	£	p	Date	Details	Folio	£	p
			PURCHASES		ACCOUNT	PA1			
					1985 Dec. 31	T. Patel	PCA1	50	00
			T. PATEL CURRENT		ACCOUNT	PCA1			
1985 Dec. 31	Purchases	PA1	50	00					

157

Current accounts with debit balances

If a partner's current account shows a debit balance it means that this partner owes the firm that amount.

Partner's current account with debit balance

		LEDGER									
DR											**CR**
Date		Details	Folio	£	p	Date		Details	Folio	£	p
			G.GREEN CURRENT ACCOUNT GCA1								
1985 Dec. 31		Drawings	D1	200	00	1985 Dec. 31		Balance	b/d	50	00
✓	✓	Purchases	PD1	100	00	✓	✓	Interest on	I1	20	00
								drawings			
								Share of profit		200	00
						✓	✓	Balance	c/d	30	00
				£300	00					£300	00
1986 Jan. 1		Balance	b/d	30	00						

This debit balance means that G. Green *owes* the firm £30.00. This will be shown in the balance sheet as a current asset.

Balance sheet extract showing partner's current account with debit balance

	BALANCE SHEET		
	as at December 31 1985		
LIABILITIES	ASSETS		
		£	£
	Fixed assets		
	Current assets		
	Stock		
	Debtors		
	Cash at bank		
	Cash in hand		
	G. Green current account		30.00

Alternative balance sheet entries for current accounts

In Chapter 11, page 154, we showed the entries in the balance sheet for the balances of the partners' current accounts.

Some partnerships require that their balance sheets show the current accounts in detail, not just the balance. As this is also often required by examining boards, here is the alternative detailed format of the liabilities side of the balance sheet given on page 154. Note how it shows the separate items contained in the partners' current accounts detailed on page 152.

Balance sheet extract of Robinson & Wainwright showing alternative presentation of partners' current accounts

ROBINSON & WAINWRIGHT — PRINTERS

BALANCE SHEET

as at August 31, 1986

LIABILITIES	£	£	£
Capital T. Robinson	7,306		
W. Wainwright	4,530	11,836	
Current accounts			
T. Robinson			
Interest on capital			
4% on 7,300	292		
Share of profit	805		
	1,097		
Less Drawings	100	997	
W. Wainwright			
Salary	100		
Share of profit	403		
	503		
Less Drawings	50	453	
Current liabilities		£	

Worked examination questions

Question 1

Iron and Stone are in partnership. Their partnership deed allows 5% per annum interest on their fixed capitals. Drawings are allowed of £3,500 Iron per annum and £2,000 Stone. They are to share profits or losses at Iron $\frac{3}{5}$ and Stone $\frac{2}{5}$.

On April 1, 1985, their fixed capital accounts were:

Iron	£8,000	Stone	£4,000

Their current accounts were:

Iron	£100 (credit)	Stone	£50 (debit)

On March 31, 1986, the profit and loss account showed a net profit of £6,000.

Prepare

- the partnership appropriation account;
- the partners' current accounts balancing these at March 31, 1986;
- the liabilities side of the balance sheet for the partnership showing the fixed capital. (The current account balances only are required.)

Solution

Partnership appropriation account

IRON & STONE

APPROPRIATION ACCOUNT

Year ended March 31, 1986

	£		£
Interest on capital		Net profit b/d from	
Iron 5% of £8,000	400.00	profit and loss account	6,000.00
Stone 5% of £4,000	200.00		
Balance being share of profit			
Iron 3/5 of £5,400	3,240.00		
Stone 2/5 of £5,400	2,160.00		
	£6,000.00		£6,000.00

160

Partners' current accounts

LEDGER

DR   **CR**

IRON CURRENT ACCOUNT ICA1

Date	Details	Folio	£	p	Date	Details	Folio	£	p
1986					1985				
Mar. 31	Drawings		3,500	00	April 1	Balance b/d		100	00
31	Balance c/d		240	00	1986				
					Mar. 31	Interest on capital		400	00
					31	Share of profit		3,240	00
			£3,740	00				£3,740	00
					1986				
					April 1	Balance b/d		240	00

STONE CURRENT ACCOUNT SCA1

Date	Details	Folio	£	p	Date	Details	Folio	£	p
1985					1986				
April 1	Balance b/d		50	00	Mar. 31	Interest on capital		200	00
1986					31	Share of profit		2,160	00
Mar. 31	Drawings		2,000	00					
Mar. 31	Balance c/d		310	00					
			£2,360	00				£2,360	00
					1986				
					April 1	Balance b/d		310	00

Extract from partnership balance sheet

IRON & STONE

BALANCE SHEET

as at April 1, 1986

LIABILITIES	£	£
Capital		
Iron	8,000	
Stone	4,000	12,000
Current accounts		
Iron	240	
Stone	310	550

Question 2

Reed and Mullen are partners who share profits and losses in the proportion of $\frac{3}{5}$ and $\frac{2}{5}$ respectively.

- Their capital accounts are : Reed   £10,000; Mullen   £8,000
- Current account balances at June 1, 1985, are: Reed   £100 (credit); Mullen   £85 (credit).
- Drawings for the year: Reed   £2,500; Mullen   £1,900.
- Interest is charged on drawings at 5%.
- Mullen is entitled to a salary of £300.
- Interest on capital is: Reed   £500; Mullen   £400.
- The net profit for the year ended May 31, 1986, is £5,700.

You are required:

- to prepare the appropriation account for the partnership; and
- to show the current account for each partner.

Solution

Partnership appropriation account

REED & MULLEN

APPROPRIATION ACCOUNT

Year ended May 31, 1986

	£	£		£
Salary			Net profit b/d from	
Mullen		300	profit & loss account	5,700
Interest on capital			Interest on drawings	
Reed	500		Reed 5% of £2,500	125
Mullen	400	900	Mullen 5% of £1,900	95
Balance being share				
of profits				
Reed 3/5 of £4,720		2,832		
Mullen 2/5 of £4,720		1,888		
		£5,920		£5,920

LEDGER

DR								**CR**
Date	Details	Folio	£	p	Date	Details	Folio	£ p

REED CURRENT ACCOUNT RCA1

Date	Details	Folio	£ p	Date	Details	Folio	£ p
1986				1985			
May 31	Drawings	D1	2,500 00	June 1	Balance b/d		100 00
31	Interest on			1986			
	drawings 5% of			June 1	Interest on capital	I1	500 00
	£2,500	I1	125 00	May 31	Share of profit		2,832 00
31	Balance c/d		807.00				
			£3,432 00	31			£3,432 00
				Jul. 1	Balance b/d		807 00

MULLEN CURRENT ACCOUNT MCA1

Date	Details	Folio	£ p	Date	Details	Folio	£ p
1986				1985			
May 31	Drawings	D2	1,900 00	June 1	Balance b/d		85 00
31	Interest on			1986			
	drawings 5% of			May 31	Interest on capital	I2	400 00
	£1,900	I2	95 00	31	Salary	S1	300 00
31	Balance c/d		678 00	31	Share of profit		1,888 00
			£2,673 00	31			£2,673 00
				1986			
				June 1	Balance b/d		678 00

Question 3

A and B are in partnership, sharing profits and losses $\frac{3}{5}$ and $\frac{2}{5}$ respectively. Each partner is to receive 5% per annum interest on their capital. A has contributed £20,000 and B £10,000. B is also to receive a salary of £1,200 per annum. On June 1, 1985, A's current account showed a credit balance of £200. B's current account had a debit balance of £100. During the year each partner drew £1,500 in cash and £500 in goods for their private use. The net trading profit for the year ended May 31, 1986 was £6,000.

Prepare:

- the appropriation section of the profit and loss account;
- A's capital and current accounts;
- B's capital and current accounts;
- show the capital and current accounts in the balance sheet (current account balances only).

Solution

Partnership appropriation account

A & B

APPROPRIATION ACCOUNT

Year ended May 31, 1986

	£		£
Salary		Net profit b/d from the	
B	1,200	profit and loss account	6,000
Interest on capital			
A: 5% of £20,000	1,000		
B: 5% of £10,000	500		
Balance being share of profit			
A: 3/5 of £3,300	1,980		
B: 2/5 of £3,300	1,320		
	£6,000		£6,000

164

LEDGER

DR   **CR**

Date	Details	Folio	£	p	Date	Details	Folio	£	p

A CAPITAL ACCOUNT ACA1

Date	Details	Folio	£ p	Date	Details	Folio	£ p
				1985 June 1	Balance	J1	£20,000 00

A CURRENT ACCOUNT ACA2

Date	Details	Folio	£ p	Date	Details	Folio	£ p
1986 May 31	Drawings	CB1	1,500 00	1985 June 1	Balance	b/d	200 00
May 31	Goods	PDB1	500 00	1986 May 31	Interest on capital		1,000 00
May 31	Balance		1,180 00	May 31	Share of profit		1,980 00
			£3,180 00				£3,180 00
				1986 June 1	Balance	b/d	1,180 00

LEDGER

DR   **CR**

Date	Details	Folio	£	p	Date	Details	Folio	£	p

B CAPITAL ACCOUNT BCA1

Date	Details	Folio	£ p	Date	Details	Folio	£ p
				1985 June 1	Balance	J1	£10,000 00

B CURRENT ACCOUNT BCA2

Date	Details	Folio	£ p	Date	Details	Folio	£ p
1985 Jun. 1	Balance	b/d	100 00	1986 May 31	Salary	AP1	1,200 00
1986 May 31	Drawings	CB1	1,500 00	May 31	Interest on capital	AP1	500 00
May 31	Goods	PDB1	500 00	May 31	Share of profit		1,320 00
May 31	Balance	c/d	920 00				
			£3,020 00				£3,020 00
				1986 Jun. 1	Balance	b/d	920 00

Extract from partnership balance sheet

A & B

BALANCE SHEET

as at May 31, 1986

LIABILITIES	£	£	ASSETS
Capital accounts			
A:	20,000		
B:	10,000	30,000	
Current accounts			
A:	1,180		
B:	920	2,100	

Chapter 12 Exercises

Partnership accounts

1 Alison and Dorothy Smythe are partners who own a hairdressing salon. Their partnership deed states:

- profits and losses are to be shared equally;
- their capitals at January 1, 1986, were: Alison £7,500; Dorothy £1,500;
- Alison is to receive a salary of £300 per annum and drawings of £300 per annum;
- Dorothy is to receive drawings of £300 per annum.

The trial balance for the year ended December 31, 1985, is as follows:

A. & D. Smythe

TRIAL BALANCE

Year ended December 31, 1985

	£	£
Stock	5,000	
Purchases	25,000	
Till receipts		38,000
Assistants' wages	2,000	
Heating/lighting	1,500	
Decorating/cleaning expenses	800	
Rates	650	
Repairs to machines and equipment	300	
Rent	500	
Debtors		
Fees due from hotel demonstrations and competitions	8,000	
Creditors		4,600
Cash at bank	7,000	
Cash in hand	250	
Capital: Alison		7,500
Dorothy		1,500
Drawings: Alison	300	
Dorothy	300	
	£51,600	£51,600

They have stock in hand at December 31 of £4,000.

You are to prepare:

- *a trading account and a profit and loss appropriation account for the year; and*
- *show the capital and current accounts for each partner, and a balance sheet for the year.*

The balances of the current accounts should be shown in the balance sheet.

2 *Chris, Catherine and Zena are partners in a tea shop. They share profits and losses in the proportion of $\frac{2}{5}$, $\frac{2}{5}$ and $\frac{1}{5}$ respectively.*

The net profit for the year ended December 31, 1985, was £7,301. Drawings are: Chris £2,000; Catherine £1,900; Zena £1,500. Interest is allowed on their capital at 6% per annum. Chris is entitled to a salary of £900 per year. Their capital accounts are: Chris £9,000; Catherine £8,000; Zena £7,000. Their current accounts showed balances of: Chris £600 (credit); Catherine £400 (debit); Zena £300 (debit).

Prepare:

- *the appropriation account;*
- *the capital and current accounts for each partner for the year ended December 31, 1985;*
- *the balance sheet extracts for the capital and current accounts (balances only required).*

3 *Choosy and Wate, stationers, are business partners who share profits and losses in the proportion of $\frac{2}{3}$ and $\frac{1}{3}$ respectively.*

The following trial balance was extracted from their books on December 31, 1985. From this you are to prepare:

- *the trading account;*
- *the profit and loss account and appropriation account;*
- *the partners' capital and current accounts;*
- *a balance sheet as at December 31, 1985, to show the balances of the partners' current accounts.*

CHOOSY & WATE
TRIAL BALANCE
Year ended December 31, 1985

	£	£
Capital accounts:		
Choosy		8,000
Wate		3,000
Current accounts:		
Choosy		500
Wate		250
Stock at January 1, 1985	4,090	
Purchases	14,020	
Sales		34,400
Wages	6,250	
Heating/lighting	2,280	
Carriage outwards	560	
Salaries (buyer and senior sales assistant)	1,500	
Repairs to fixtures & fittings	1,628	
Rates	370	
Premises	4,010	
Fixtures and fittings	8,800	
Drawings: Choosy	2,700	
Wate	1,700	
Cash at bank (overdrawn)		3,998
Cash in hand	220	
Debtors	4,500	
Creditors		2,950
Decorating of showroom	470	
	£53,098	£53,098

Notes:

- Stock in hand at December 31, 1985, £4,670.
- Rates paid in advance £40.
- Depreciate fixtures and fittings by £400.
- The partners are entitled to interest on their capital at 5% per annum.
- Wate is to receive a salary of £450.

4 E. Allison and E. Welsh are partners sharing profits and losses: E. Allison $\frac{3}{5}$; E. Welsh $\frac{2}{5}$.

On September 1, 1985, their fixed capital accounts were: E. Allison £7,000; E. Welsh £3,000.

Their current account balances were: E. Allison £250 (credit); E. Welsh £100 (credit). Their partnership agreement states that they are each to receive 5% per annum interest on their capital.

Their drawings for the year ended August 31, 1985, were: E. Allison £4,000; E. Welsh £2,500.

- Prepare a profit and loss appropriation account showing the net profit for the year as £6,240.
- Prepare the current accounts of the partners as at August 31, 1985.

5 Mathews, Bradley and Colvin are partners who share profits in the proportion of their capitals. Their capitals are £5,000, £2,000 and £1,000 respectively. The net profit for the year ended December 31, 1985, was £7,200. Interest on capital is to be allowed at 5% per annum, and Bradley is to have a salary of £300.

Show the division of the profit by means of the appropriation account.

Answers are given in the Worked Solutions.

13 Manufacturing Accounts

From the beginning of his business Tom Robinson regularly had to buy in stocks of paper, inks, cleaning fluids, etc., so that he could work as a printer. Some of the early entries in his books read as follows:

The credit entry in Tom's cash book

DR					CASH	BOOK		CB1			CR
		RECEIPTS						PAYMENTS			
Date	Details	Folio	Discount Allowed	Cash	Bank	Date	Details	Folio	Discount Received	Cash	Bank
						Sept. 3	D. Clarke	C1.			80.00

A debit entry in Tom's ledger

			D. Clarke C 1.								
DR											CR
Date	Details		Folio	£	p	Date	Details		Folio	£	p
Sept. 3	Bank		CB1	80	00						

D. Clarke owns a small factory which specialises in the production of inks and other fluids supplying the printing trade. He is a manufacturer, which means he purchases raw materials and by using labour and machinery changes these materials into finished products which he sells at a profit. The raw materials in this instance are resins, dyes, viscous liquids and other additives which go into the making of inks needed by printers.

As a manufacturer he needs to keep a record of the cost of production of the articles produced during the trading period. To do this an account called a **manufacturing account** is prepared before the trading account in a manufacturing business.

In a manufacturing account it is important to group the expenses in set stages on the debit side:

1)   the **direct** or **variable costs**;
2)   the **indirect** or **fixed costs**;
3)   **work in progress**.

The direct or variable costs

The types of cost which can vary in manufacturing are the price of the raw materials and the wages which are paid to the workers. The cost of raw materials, for example, will fluctuate with other market prices, and the cost of wages will vary with the amount of overtime, etc., which may have to be worked. It follows that the variable costs will increase with increased production.

The following direct or variable costs will be entered on the debit side of the manufacturing account:

- the stocks of raw materials at the start;
- the cost of raw materials purchased during the trading period, *less* returns outward;
- *less* stock of raw materials unused at the end of the period;
- *add* carriage inward of raw materials (road, rail, freight);
- *add* wages paid to the workers who produce the goods.

All these items make up the **prime cost** of manufacturing.

The indirect or fixed costs

These are overhead and factory costs. They relate to the expenses which are necessary to operate the factory and are payable independent of production. They include a variety of expenses such as rent, rates, the salary of the works manager, repairs, and depreciation of the machines and of the building. These expenses are considered to be 'fixed' or constant, usually remaining the same for at least a year. They are listed and added to the prime costs.

Work in progress

Products which are only partly completed at the time the manufacturing account is being prepared are classed as *work in progress*.

We need to have two figures for the work in progress. The first is the value of the work in progress at the beginning of the period, and this amount is added to the total of the direct and indirect costs.

The second figure is the value of the work in progress at the end of the period when the manufacturing account is prepared. This must be deducted from the total of all the above to give us the final cost of finished goods.

The manufacturing account

We will now prepare D. Clarke's manufacturing account showing all these costs in their separate groups. The following balances were extracted from the ledger on December 30, 1985:

Stock of dyes, resins, etc., at January 1, 1985	£5,272
Stock of dyes, resins, etc., at December 31, 1985	£3,150
*Raw materials purchased during the year	£7,420
*Returns outward	£210
*Carriage inward of raw materials	£125
Manufacturing wages	£12,000
Factory rent and rates	£1,874
Power and light	£700
Machinery cost (to be depreciated by 10%)	£1,200
Work in progress:	
Partly manufactured goods at January 1, 1985	£3,000
Partly manufactured goods at December 31, 1985	£1,450

D. Clarke & Co.
MANUFACTURING ACCOUNT (Debit side)
year ended 31 December, 1985

Dr			Cr
	£	£	
Raw materials			
Stocks of dyes, resins & additives at Jan. 1, 1985		5,272	
Purchases	7,420		
Less Returns	210	7,210	
		12,482	
Carriage inwards		125	
		12,607	

(*These costs would be subject to VAT at the standard rate (15%). The amounts would be shown in the VAT input account.)

Less stock at Dec. 31, 1985	3,150
	9,457
Manufacturing wages	12,000
Prime cost	£21,457
Factory overheads	
Rent and rates	1,874
Power/light	700
10% depreciation of machinery (cost £1,200)	120
Work in progress at Jan. 1, 1985	3,000
	27,151
Less work in progress at Dec. 31, 1985	1,450
Cost of production of finished goods	£25,701

The cost of production for the year is £25,701 on the *debit* side. To balance the account the *credit* entry for the above will be:

D. Clarke & Co.
MANUFACTURING ACCOUNT
Year ended December 31, 1985

Dr				Cr
			Cost of production transferred to trading account	25,701
Cost of production	£25,701			£25,701

The final accounts

Assuming that the following extracts have been taken from D. Clarke's ledger we will prepare the trading and profit and loss accounts.

Stock of finished goods at January 1, 1985	£10,000
Stock of finished goods at December 31, 1985	£7,265
Sales for the year	£70,300
Office salaries	£6,000
Rent and rates	£2,200
Cleaning and decorating	£2,300
Telephone	£400
Sundry expenses	£250

D. Clarke & Co.
TRADING ACCOUNT
Year ended December 31, 1985

	£		£
Finished goods		Sales	70,300*
Stock at Jan. 1, 1985	10,000		
Cost of production	25,701		
	35,701		
Less stock at Dec. 31, 1985	7,265		
Cost of goods sold	28,436		
Balance being gross profit c/d to profit and loss account	41,864		
	£70,300		£70,300

*VAT at 15% will have been charged on these sales and recorded in the VAT output account since the turnover is more than that required for registration for VAT (see Chapter 3).

In the preceding trading account we have omitted an entry for 'purchases' and replaced it with 'cost of production'. This is because during the year for which the manufacturing account has been prepared the firm produced from its own raw materials sufficient goods to satisfy the demand (orders) from its customers. If D. Clarke & Co. had not been able to fulfil all the orders then it would have been necessary to buy in finished products from other firms to meet the deficiency.

D. Clarke & Co.
PROFIT AND LOSS ACCOUNT
Year ended December 31, 1985

	£		£
Office salaries	6,000	Gross profit b/d from trading account	41,864
Rent & rates	2,200		
Cleaning/decorating	2,300		
Sundry expenses	250		
Telephone	400		
Balance being net profit for the year	30,714		
	£41,864		£41,864

The balance sheet at December 31 would be presented in either the vertical or horizontal style, but the current assets would include:

D. Clarke & Co.
BALANCE SHEET
as at December 31, 1985

	Current assets	£
	Stock of raw materials at 31 Dec., 1985	3,150
	Work in progress	1,450
	Stock of finished goods	7,265

Manufacturing profit

From the profit and loss account D. Clarke now knows how much profit he has made by producing and selling his own products. It does not, however, show the *manufacturing* profit, that is the profit obtained by using his own raw materials. He needs to know this in order to compare it with that of purchasing the finished products from another manufacturer. This will show if it is to his advantage to have a factory producing the goods from the raw materials.

He must first either estimate or find out by investigation what the current trade or market price is of his finished goods. Let us say he discovers that the trade price is £31,112. He has produced them for £25,701, a gross profit on manufacturing of £5,411.

To show this profit and the trade price for comparative purposes in the manufacturing and profit and loss accounts the following adjustments are made:

1)   The manufacturing account:

D. Clarke & Co.
MANUFACTURING ACCOUNT
Year ended Dec. 31, 1985

Dr			Cr
	£		£
Cost of production	25,701	Trade price of finished goods	31,112
Balance being gross manufacturing profit c/d to profit and loss account	5,411		
	£31,112		£31,112

2)   In the trading account this trade price (*not* the cost price) is transferred to the debit side.

This is shown on the next page.

D. Clarke & Co.
TRADING ACCOUNT
year ended December 31, 1985

	£		£
Finished goods			
Stock at Jan. 1, 1985	10,000	Sales	70,300
Trade price b/d from manufacturing account	31,112		
	41,112		
Less stock at Dec. 31, 1985	7,265		
Cost of goods sold	33,847		
Balance being gross profit c/d to profit and loss account	36,453		
	£70,300		£70,300

3) In the profit and loss account:

D. Clarke & Co.
PROFIT AND LOSS ACCOUNT
year ended December 31, 1985

	£		£
Office salaries	6,000	Gross profit on manufacturing	5,411
Rent and rates	2,200	Gross profit on sales b/d from trading account	36,453
Cleaning/decorating	2,300		
Sundry expenses	250		
Telephone	400		
Balance being net profit c/d to balance sheet	30,714		
	£41,864		£41,864

The net profit has remained the same but the gross profit made by manufacturing his own goods is good reason enough for D. Clarke to retain the factory.

Chapter 13 Exercises

1 *From the following balances extracted from the books of the Gelatino Ice Cream Manufacturing Company at the year ended June 30, 1986 prepare a manufacturing account, a trading account and a profit and loss account, and show the current assets in the balance sheet as at that date.*

Stocks of raw materials at July 1, 1985	£2,200
Purchases of raw materials during the year	£21,400
Carriage inwards – raw materials	£422
Stocks of raw materials at June 30, 1986	£3,200
Manufacturing wages	£20,000
Work in progress at July 1, 1985	£3,000
Work in progress at June 30, 1986	£4,200
Factory power	£2,100
Repairs to machines	£1,500
Depreciation of machines	£500
Trade price of finished goods	£70,000
Stocks of finished ice cream packs at July 1, 1985	£9,800
Sales	£102,400
Purchases of finished ice cream packs	£11,200
Returns outward	£50
Stocks of ice cream packs at June 30, 1986	£10,500
Various office expenses	£11,500
Office rent	£2,000
Stationery	£602
Telephone	£222

2 *From the following balances prepare the manufacturing and trading accounts for the Rossi Candle Manufacturing Company for the year ended December, 31 1985.*
Prepare the accounts to show clearly

- *the cost of finished goods manufactured;*
- *the cost of goods sold.*

Stocks at January 1, 1985	
Raw materials	£2,430
Work in progress	£3,623
Finished goods	£7,074
Purchases of raw materials	£28,356
Factory wages	£23,330
Wages due	£520
Factory cleaning/rent	£1,026
Factory lighting/heating	£4,215
Factory power	£584

Stocks at December 31, 1985

Raw materials	£2,581
Work in progress	£3,447
Stock of finished goods in hand	£7,368
Sales for the year	£106,209

Note: Factory machines cost £14,000. These must be depreciated by 10%.

3 *The balances below have been taken from the books of T. Ho Cardboard Carton manufacturers for the year ended December 31, 1985. You are to prepare:*

- *the manufacturing account;*
- *a trading account and profit and loss account dated December 31, 1985;*
- *a balance sheet as at that date.*

You have been given the following additional information which must be included in the accounts:

- stocks of raw materials at December 31, 1985   £1,632
- stocks of finished goods at December 31, 1985   £3,024
- work in progress at December 31, 1985   £4,250
- trade price of finished goods   £40,198
- machinery is to be depreciated by 10% on cost.

	£	£	£
Stocks of raw materials at January 1, 1985		1,356	
Stock of finished goods at January 1, 1985		3,654	
Work in progress at January 1, 1985		3,000	
Purchases raw materials		16,263	
Factory wages		14,062	
Rates – factory	2,184		
office	3,186	5,370	
Factory – light/heat		772	
power		1,000	
Office – expenses		1,654	
salaries		6,900	
Machinery cost		16,000	
Premises		13,125	
Sales			67,000
Debtors		7,500	
Creditors			2,549
Bank		4,614	
Drawings		6,500	
Capital at January, 1985			32,221
		£101,770	£101,770

180

4 *The balances in L. Lenick's books on March 31, 1986 were as follows:*

	£	£
Stocks of raw materials at April 1, 1985	20,000	
Purchases of raw materials for the year	115,840	
Work in progress at April 1, 1985	4,200	
Stocks of finished goods at April 1, 1985	26,880	
Sales		186,562
Plant and machinery (cost)	47,600	
Office equipment	9,600	
Factory wages	17,280	
Office salaries	9,280	
Advertising and packages	5,120	
Factory – heating/lighting	8,720	
power	4,000	
rates and insurance	2,000	
Returns outward – raw materials		620
Office expenses	6,160	

Prepare:

- *the manufacturing account showing the prime cost and the cost of production;*
- *the trading account, showing the cost of goods sold;*
- *the profit and loss account.*

The following details must also be included in the appropriate accounts:

- stocks of raw materials at March 31, 1986: £21,520
- stocks of finished goods £29,800
- the machines are to be depreciated by 15% on cost
- the office equipment is to be depreciated by 10%
- work in progress at March 31, 1986 £2,490

Answers are given in the *Worked Solutions.*

14 Departmental Accounts

Where a business has more than one department it is usual for the owner to keep separate records for each department's transactions. This allows for comparisons to be made showing the profitability or otherwise between the departments and the business as a whole. The final accounts may well show a satisfactory profit taken as a whole, but one department could be running at a loss. Departmental records therefore help in the analysis of the figures.

In order to record the separate figures extra columns called **analysis columns** are introduced into the day books and the ledger.

If we return to Tom Robinson's printing business we find that he has now divided the printing section into two departments: Department A prints and sells posters, letterheads and general commercial stationery; Department B prints and sells magazines. We will also introduce VAT columns in our analysis sheets of the day books. Department A requires VAT to be shown, the standard rate being 15% (as at 1987). Department B, which produces magazines, is zero rated and is not subject to output VAT (as at 1986) but pays input VAT on purchases and carriage inwards in the same way as Department A.

The departmental purchases day book

The rulings and headings will be:

				Dept. A		Dept. B		Total	
Date	Details	Invoice No	Folio	Net	Input VAT	Net	Input VAT	Net	VAT

DEPARTMENTAL PURCHASES DAY BOOK PDB1

- A total column is necessary in order to prove that the amounts shown are accurately recorded.

The departmental sales day book

				Dept. A		Dept. B		Total	
				DEPARTMENTAL SALES DAY BOOK SDB1					
Date	Details	Invoice No	Folio	Net	Output VAT	Net	Output VAT	Net	VAT

- *Department A* purchases for printing and selling posters, letter heads and commercial stationery must have separate columns for input VAT. This is at the standard rate (15% as at 1986).
- *Department B* is not subject to VAT output on sales because magazines and books are zero rated as at 1986. However, in the layout of the sales day book a column is printed for output VAT to provide for *possible* changes in future VAT requirements.

The departmental ledger showing the stock account

STOCK ACCOUNT SA1

DR									**CR**
Date	Details	Folio	Dept. A	Dept. B	Date	Details	Folio	Dept. A	Dept. B
1985					1986				
June 1	Balance	b/d	2,108	3,164	May 31	Trading account	J1	1,478	644
					✔ 31	Balance	c/d	630	2,520
			£2,108	£3,164				£2,108	£3,164
June 1	Balance	b/d	630	2,520					

The departmental trading account

We will assume the following figures have been extracted from Tom's ledger for the year ended June 30, 1986:

| | Input VAT @ 15% | | | |
	Dept A	Dept B	Dept A	Dept B
Opening stock			£2,108	£3,164
Closing stock			£630	£2,520
Purchases	£376	£564	£2,508	£3,761
Carriage in	£13	£3	£87	£22
Wages			£2,800	£2,000
Total sales			£19,262*	£20,434

We will now prepare Tom's trading account.

DEPARTMENTAL TRADING ACCOUNT
year ended June 30, 1986

	Dept. A	Dept. B	Total		Dept. A	Dept. B	Total
	£	£	£		£	£	£
Stock at July 1 1985	2,108	3,164	5,272	Sales	19,262	20,434	39,696
Purchases	2,508	3,761	6,269				
Carriage in	87	22	109				
	4,703	6,947	11,650				
Wages	2,800	2,000	4,800				
	7,503	8,947	16,450				
Less Stock at June 30, 1986	630	2,520	3,150				
Cost of goods sold	6,873	6,427	13,300				
Balance being gross profit c/d to trading account	12,389	14,007	26,396				
	£19,262	£20,434	£39,696		£19,262	£20,434	£39,696

*May not be subject to VAT as the threshold has not been reached.

The departmental profit and loss account

We will assume that the revenue expenses for Tom Robinson's business are:

	£
Rent for showroom and workroom – 50% each department	1,600
Rates – 50% each department	520
Lighting/heating – 60% and 40%	800
Power – 50% each department	650
Cleaning of premises – 60% and 40%	400
Telephones – 60% and 40%	325
Salary – showroom manageress	2,000
Depreciation of machinery – Dept A £137, Dept B £138	275
Depreciation – showroom fixtures & fittings Dept B	100

Rent and rates

In practice rent and rates are apportioned by the area of floor space occupied by each department. We are assuming that each department has the same area of floor space allocated.

Lighting and heating

This is apportioned by the number of electricity points fitted in each department. Power for production in this departmental profit and loss account will be divided equally between the departments because the same machines are used for each kind of job. This will not apply in larger firms.

VAT account

INPUT VAT ACCOUNT V1									
DR									**CR**
Date	Details	Folio	Dept. A	Dept. B	Date	Details	Folio	Dept. A	Dept. B
1986									
June 30	Purchases	B1	376	564					
30	Carr. In	C1	13	3					

The balances from the input VAT account for each department are shown in the profit and loss account.

DEPARTMENTAL PROFIT AND LOSS ACCOUNT
year ended June 30, 1986

	Dept. A	Dept. B	Total		Dept. A	Dept. B	Total
	£	£	£		£	£	£
Rent (50% each)	800	800	1,600	Gross profit b/d from trading a/c	12,389	14,007	26,396
Rates (50% each)	260	260	520				
Light/heat (3/5:2/5)	480	320	800				
Power (50% each)	325	325	650				
Cleaning (3/5:2/5)	240	160	400				
Telephones (3/5:2/5)	195	130	325				
Salary P/T		2,000	2,000				
Input VAT	389	567	956				
Depreciation							
Machinery	137	138	275				
S/room fittings		100	100				
Balance being profit c/d to balance sheet	9,563	9,207	18,770				
	£12,389	£14,007	£26,396		£12,389	£14,007	£26,396

The departmental balance sheet

The balance sheet entries for each department's stock in hand and the net profit for the year will be:

BALANCE SHEET
as at June 30, 1986

		£	£			£
Net profit	Dept. A	9,563		Current Assets		630
	Dept. B	9,207		Stock	Dept. A	2,520
					Dept. B	3,150

Chapter 14 Exercises

1 *The Luxury Laundry & Cleaning Co. have extracted the following balances from their books in order to prepare a trading and profit and loss account showing the gross and net profits for each department for the month ended March 31, 1986. Ignore VAT.*

	Cleaning	Laundry
Stock of materials at March 1, 1986	£6,600	£4,500
Stock at March 31, 1986	£3,200	£4,000
Sales	£14,400	£9,600
Purchases	£7,890	£7,200
Salaries	£1,875	£1,248
Rent and rates	£695	
Telephone	£159	
General expenses	£230	

- Rent and rates are to be divided $\frac{2}{5}$ and $\frac{3}{5}$.
- Telephone is to be divided $\frac{2}{3}$ and $\frac{1}{3}$.
- General expenses are to be divided $\frac{1}{2}$ and $\frac{1}{2}$.

2 *The Grotto Toy Shop has three departments: soft toys, mechanical toys, and games.*

Prepare an input VAT account, an output VAT account, a departmental trading account and profit and loss account from the following balances, year ended December 31, 1985.

	Soft toys £	Mechanical toys £	Games £
Stocks at January 1, 1985	6,000	12,000	8,000
Sales	22,500	30,522	42,200
Output VAT @ 15%	3,375	4,578	6,330
Purchases	8,500	4,522	12,200
Input VAT @ 15%	1,275	678	1,830
Wages	3,000	2,500	4,225
Advertising	500	500	500
Rent and rates	2,300	1,150	1,150
Heating and lighting	1,103	1,103	1,103
Administration expenses	1,500	1,500	1,000
Canteen	1,000	1,000	1,000
Stocks at December 31, 1985	3,500	5,000	2,620

3 *The Music Centre has three departments: sheet music, records and tapes.*

From the following information prepare a departmental trading and profit and loss account for the year ended March 31, 1986. Ignore VAT.

	Sheet Music	Records	Tapes
	£	£	£
Stocks at April 1, 1985	800	4,500	6,600
Sales	3,000	20,000	28,800
Purchases	1,200	9,000	12,000
Wages	500	2,300	2,700
Salaries	400	1,950	1,470
Rent and insurance	147	650	680
Shop expenses	220	1,416	3,822
Depreciation of fixtures and equipment	100	250	600
Stocks at March 31, 1986	600	3,300	4,200

4 *The Dairy Products Shop has three departments: butter, cheese and fresh cream products. Ignore VAT.*

Prepare a departmental trading account and profit and loss account from the following information for the year ended December 31, 1985.

	Butter	Cheese	Fresh cream products
	£	£	£
Stocks at January 1, 1985	1,200	27,800	33,000
Stocks at December 31, 1985	1,500	13,000	32,000
Sales	13,400	53,040	38,350
Purchases	5,600	14,400	20,000
Wages	2,700	11,600	8,500
Salaries	3,000	9,500	4,200
Rates	150	600	760
General expenses	360	1,030	1,620

Answers are given in the *Worked Solutions.*

15 Non-profit Making Organisations

Our attention throughout this text has been concentrated on what is the most common type of business – one which exists in order to make a profit for the owner. We have followed the fortunes of Tom Robinson, from the beginning of his firm to the establishment of his partnership with W. Wainwright, always with the aim of recording the financial stability of the business.

However, there are other organisations which need to be run on a business-like basis, but which are not concerned with making a profit. Voluntary bodies, charities, sports and social clubs, etc., are all groups which have been formed to carry out some particular activity or service. Normally, such organisations raise money by subscriptions (or contributions) from members or by special fund-raising events, and whatever monies they possess are used to carry out the purpose of the organisation – not for making a profit. But they do need to keep a record of their finances to make sure that the organisation is not running into debt.

Let us continue with our friend Tom. Aside from his work as a printer we find that in his spare time he is an enthusiastic member of a local amateur dramatic society, the Tynecastle Players. Because of his business experience, Tom acts as honorary treasurer (unpaid) for the society.

The Tynecastle Players were formed on January 2, 1985. There are 80 full-time members each paying £5 per annum as subscriptions. There are also 100 associate members paying £2 per annum for the privilege. Thus the annual income from subscriptions is £600. The society has a weekly meeting in a room in the local community centre for which £50 per annum is charged as rent. In addition to the subscriptions they also organise a number of coffee evenings and wine and cheese parties which raise a further £500 during the year.

The society has two productions, one in March and one in October. In March they sold tickets to the value of £350 and also programmes worth £50. In October they sold tickets valued at £450 and programmes valued at £85. For both these shows they had to pay for the hire of a hall which cost £500 for each show. The cost of printing tickets and programmes was £20 (because of Tom's connections they got them very cheaply). They also had to pay for the professional services of an electrician and a stagehand which cost £25 for each production.

The hire of costumes and scenery cost £125, which included a deposit of £25 which was refunded when the costumes were returned.

Every time the society met there were refreshments provided. Over the year these cost £80, and £95 was raised from their sale.

The receipts and payments account

As treasurer Tom has to keep a record of all the above items. Unlike his business, he does not need to keep a double entry system of book-keeping. It will be sufficient if he has a cash book. He will summarise the various items in the cash book under several headings from which he will prepare a **receipts and payments account**.

This is an account which shows a summary of all the society's *cash* transactions recorded in a cash book which has columns to correspond with the various transactions. For example, it could have columns on the receipts side for subscriptions, income from various social functions, shows, etc., and on the payments side columns for expenses such as wages, printing, rent, etc.

The Tynecastle Players' cash book would most likely have columns as follows:

Cash book rulings for the Tynecastle Players

DR						RECEIPTS				
Date	Supplier	Ref.	Total	Subscriptions	Cheese/wine	Tickets	Programmes	Shows Refreshments	Sundries

				PAYMENTS						CR
Date	Supplier	Ref.	Total	Printing	Wages	Rent	Theatre	Costumes	Shows Refreshments	Sundries

At the end of the financial year the cash book would be balanced and the total of each column would be shown in a receipts and payments account.

The receipts and payments account below contains a record of the Tynecastle Players Amateur Dramatic Society's accounts.

Receipts and payments account for the Tynecastle Players

TYNECASTLE PLAYERS

RECEIPTS AND PAYMENTS ACCOUNT

Year ended December 31, 1985

RECEIPTS	£	PAYMENTS	£
Subscriptions			
Full-time members 60 @ £5	300	Hire of theatre 2 shows	1,000
Associate members 80 @ £2	160	Printing	20
Wine and cheese parties	500	Costumes	125
Coffee mornings		Refreshments	80
		Electrician & stagehand	50
Shows		Rent	50
March: Tickets	350		
Programmes	50	Balance	
October: Tickets	450	Bank	650
Programmes	85	Cash	40
Deposit refund for costumes	25		
Refreshments	95		
	£2,015		£2,015

Tom, however, realises this is not a complete picture of the society's finances. As in every group, for example, there are bound to be members who do not pay their subscriptions. The following items are therefore found to be still outstanding:

1) Subscriptions

		£
• Full-time members: 20 still outstanding (20 × £5)		100.00
• Associate members: 20 still outstanding (20 × £2)		40.00
2) Costume cleaning account outstanding		30.00
3) Insurance		15.00
4) Performing rights for two shows @ £10 per show		20.00

To include the above items, and to give an accurate picture of the society's finances, Tom needs to prepare an **income and expenditure account.**.

The income and expenditure account

This is an account which is similar to a profit and loss account. It is given the special heading income and expenditure account because, as has already been noted, non-profit making organisations do not aim at making a profit.

In drawing up an income and expenditure account the following method is used:

- *On the debit side*

  1) all the expenses
  2) adjustments for expenses outstanding at the end of the year
  3) the balance when it is a gain.

- *On the credit side*

  1) all the receipts
  2) payments made in advance
  3) the balance when it is a loss.

The income and expenditure account for the Tynecastle Players is given on the next page.

TYNECASTLE PLAYERS

INCOME AND EXPENDITURE ACCOUNT

Year ended 31 December, 1985

EXPENSES	£	£	INCOME	£	£
Hire of theatre		1,000	Refreshments	95	
Printing		20	Less Cost	80	
					15
Costumes					
Hire	125		Subscriptions		
Less Refund	25		Full-time members	300	
	100		Add Due 20 × £5	100	
Cleaning	30				400
		130	Associated members	160	
			Add Due 20 × £2	40	
					200
Wages					
Electrician/stagehand		50	Socials		
Rent		50	Coffee/cheese & wine		500
Insurance		15			
Performing rights (2 shows)		20	Tickets		
Balance being			March	350	
excess of income over			October	450	
expenditure for the year		765			800
			Programmes		
			March	50	
			October	85	
					135
		£2,050			£2,050

The balance sheet

Immediately after the New Year the Tynecastle Players will hold its annual general meeting. Tom will now produce the balance sheet as the final statement of the society's activities for the year. This will enable the members to see exactly how they stand, and also allow them to decide how much they can afford to donate to charity as a result of their endeavours. Obviously the society will need to keep a certain amount of money to ensure their next year's programme can go ahead.

The balance sheet for the Tynecastle Players will look as follows.

The Tynecastle Players' balance sheet

TYNECASTLE PLAYERS AMATEUR DRAMATIC SOCIETY

BALANCE SHEET

as at December 31, 1985

	£		£	£
General fund		**Current assets**		
Being excess of income		Subscriptions in arrears:		
over expenditure for		Full-time members	100	
the year	765	Associate members	40	
				140
Current liabilities		Cash at bank	650	
Costumes (cleaning)	30	Cash in hand	40	
Insurance	15			690
Performing rights (2 shows)	20			
	£830			**£830**

I certify that the above accounts are an accurate record of the financial affairs of Tynecastle Players Amateur Dramatic Society.

Signed

Treasurer

Auditor

Date

The general fund

In the Tynecastle Players' balance sheet shown above the first item on the liabilities side is given as the **general fund**. This is sometimes called the **accumulated fund**. It represents the net worth of the organisation – the assets minus the liabilities at the start of the club's activities. Each year any surplus of income over expenditure is *added* to this general fund. Equally, if there has been a loss during the year, then that will be *deducted* from the general fund.

In the case of the Tynecastle Players there was no general fund when the society first started. For them, the general fund began with the excess income over expenditure at the end of the first year.

Let us look at another example of how a general fund (capital) is arrived at.

Example

On January 1, 1986, the Dunelm Squash Club owned premises of £5,000 with furniture and fittings in the clubrooms of £2,500. The bank balance was £2,000, with cash in hand at £60. The subscriptions of 40 members at £2 each were in arrears, and a bill for £100 for repairs to the premises is still awaiting payment.

We need to find the club's general fund (capital) at the start of its activities:

Method

	£
Assets:	
Premises	5,000
Furniture and fittings	2,500
Cash at bank	2,000
Cash in hand	60
Subscriptions in arrears	80
	£9,640
Less Liabilities:	
Repairs	100
The general fund is	£9,540

The general fund is shown as the first item on the liabilities side of the balance sheet as indicated on page 198.

Worked example

The Gatehouse Camping Club owned the following items on January 1, 1985.

	£
Camping equipment valued at	8,000
Furniture and fittings in the club	2,000
A typewriter	200
A TV set	250
Balance at the bank	550
Cash in hand	60

1) You are required to find the general fund for this club.
2) Prepare an income and expenditure account from the following receipts and payments account.
3) Prepare the balance sheet as at December 31, 1985.

THE GATEHOUSE CAMPING CLUB

RECEIPTS AND PAYMENTS ACCOUNT

Year ended December 31, 1985

RECEIPTS	£	PAYMENTS	£
Balance at bank Jan. 1, 1985	550	Rent of clubhouse	1,300
Cash in hand	60	Rates	150
Subscriptions	600	Repairs to equipment	120
Receipts for hire/equipment	1260	New tents	275
Camping fees	900	Social expenses	70
Sale of social tickets	180	Wages: Warden	300
		Greenkeepers	200
		Balance at bank	1,135
	£3,550		£3,550

- Of the £600 subscriptions £60 has been paid in advance for 1986.

- The camping equipment, value £8,000 on January 1, 1985, must be depreciated by 5%.

- The water rate of £10 has not been paid.

Solution

1) *The general fund:*

	£
Camping equipment	8,000
Furniture and fittings	2,000
Typewriter	200
TV set	250
Cash at bank	550
Cash in hand	60
	£11,060

2) *The income and expenditure account:*

THE GATEHOUSE CAMPING CLUB
INCOME AND EXPENDITURE ACCOUNT
Year ended December 31, 1985

EXPENSES	£	£	INCOME	£	£
Rent of clubhouse		1,300	Subscriptions	600	
Rates	150		Less Advance	60	
Add Water rate	10				540
		160	Hire of equipment		1,260
Repairs to equipment		120	Camping fees		900
Wages: Warden		300	Sale of social tickets	180	
Greenkeeper		200	Less Expenses	70	
					110
Depreciation:					
Camping equipment					
5% of £8,000		400			
Balance being excess of					
income over expenditure		330			
		£2,810			£2,810

- When a profit has been made on a social function the *net* figure must be shown in the *income* section. If, however, the result is a loss then expenses are shown on the *expenses* side and the income on the *income side*.
- Notice that the depreciation of the camping equipment is to be based on 5% of the value *at the start of the year* – 5% of £8,000. The new tents are *not* included in the depreciation in this exercise.
- The depreciation is also shown in the balance sheet under fixed assets (see page 198).

3) *The balance sheet:*

THE GATEHOUSE CAMPING CLUB
BALANCE SHEET
As at December, 31, 1985

	£	£		£	£
General fund	11,060		**Fixed Assets**		
Add Excess income over expenditure for 1985	330	11,390	Camping equipment Less Depreciation @ 5%	8,000 400	7,600
Current liabilities			Add New tents		275
Water rate (due)		10	Furniture and Fittings		2,000
Subscriptions in advance		60	Typewriter		200
			TV set		250
					10,325
			Current assets		
			Cash at bank		1,135
		£11,460			£11,460

- Subscriptions in advance are a *liability* because the club has received the money but the members have not yet received the facilities (the subscriptions cover the following year). Therefore the club *owes* the facilities to the members, i.e. it is in *debt* to them, until they have enjoyed the facilities they have already paid for.
- Any subscriptions in arrears would be shown as a *current asset*. The club is fortunate that there are no subscriptions in arrears and everyone has paid up to date. Had there been any arrears these would be shown as current assets because the members would be in debt to the club.

Chapter 15 Exercises

Non-profit making organisations

1 *The Hillsview Disco Club was formed on January 1, 1985. Admission is by ticket only, payable at the door.*

The club had the following assets when they started:

Music centres valued	£700
Tapes, recording and lighting equipment	£2,000
Seats and furniture	£1,000
Bank balance	£250

At the end of their first financial year, the secretary presented the receipts and payments account for the club:

HILLSVIEW DISCO CLUB
RECEIPTS AND PAYMENTS ACCOUNT
Year ended December 31, 1985

RECEIPTS	£	PAYMENTS	£
Bank balance	250	Rent	200
Entrance money	1,500	New equipment	1,250
Disco competitions	620	Secretary's expenses	150
'Pop-Hit' magazine sales	615	Disco competitions	505
'Come as You Please' social	245	'Pop-Hit' magazine costs	175
		'Come as You Please' social prizes	50
		Balance at bank	900
	£3,230		**£3,230**

You have been asked to prepare:

- *the general fund;*
- *an income and expenditure account for the year;*
- *a balance sheet as at December 31, 1985.*

The secretary advises you that, in addition to the expenses he has recorded, there is an outstanding account for printing expenses of £16. The furniture is to be depreciated by 10% and the recording equipment etc., value £2,000, is to be depreciated by £200. Rent paid in advance is £63.

199

2 *The Northumbrian Classical Music Society's treasurer prepared the following receipts and payments account for the year ended March 31, 1986:*

THE NORTHUMBRIAN CLASSICAL MUSIC SOCIETY

RECEIPTS AND PAYMENTS ACCOUNT

Year ended March 31, 1986

RECEIPTS	£	PAYMENTS	£
Balance at bank 30 April 1985	160	Travelling expenses	240
Subscriptions	128	Secretary's expenses	35
Concert receipts	180	Rent of meeting room	103
Hire of instruments to members	135	Visiting lecturers	25
		Hire of overhead projector	10
		Concert expenses	83
		Balance	107
	£603		£603

The club's general fund at the start of the year was £1,070.

The assets were:

- Cash   £160
- Instruments   £250
- A mini-bus   £650
- Subscriptions unpaid   £10

You are required to prepare the income and expenditure account for the year ended March 31, 1986, and a balance sheet as at that date, also taking the following into account.

- *The club has 56 members and the annual subscription is £2 each.*
- *The £10 subscriptions which were outstanding for the previous year were paid in February.*
- *The mini-bus is to be depreciated by 10%.*
- *A bill for repairs to instruments of £15 has not been paid.*

3 *Below is the receipts and payments account of the Windsmoor Cricket Club for the year ended December 31, 1985.*

WINDSMOOR CRICKET CLUB

RECEIPTS AND PAYMENTS ACCOUNT

Year ended December 31, 1985

RECEIPTS	£	PAYMENTS	£
Balance at bank Jan. 1, 1985	1,170	Groundsman's wages	400
Subscriptions	1,700	Upkeep of pitches	640
Fees	350	Water rate	25
Donations from patrons	280	Printing and stationery	125
Concerts/social functions	650	Postages, telephone etc.	160
		Balance at bank	2,800
	£4,150		£4,150

The following accounts are still outstanding:

Stationery	£8
Rent owing	£211
Subscriptions due	£80

The club also had the following assets at January 1, 1985:

Clubhouse	£3,560
Equipment and furniture	£4,500
Balance at bank	£1,170

You are to prepare:

- *the general fund;*
- *an income and expenditure account for the year;*
- *a balance sheet.*

Answers are given in the *Worked Solutions.*

16 Preparation of Final Accounts from Incomplete Records

In Chapter 15 we found out that Tom Robinson was appointed honorary treasurer of the local amateur dramatic society, where his business experience proved invaluable in keeping the society's financial activities as successful as their stage productions.

Tom's advice was often sought too by his friends and associates. On one occasion Mandy and Penny Tiptree, also members of the society, brought their business problems to him (together with lots of invoices, receipted bills and a notebook showing how much they had drawn from the business for their personal use). They needed his help.

At the beginning of the year (January 1, 1985) they had rented an attractive shop in the market square. Full of enthusiasm they started a business selling high class cosmetics and perfumes. Between them they had several years of experience in the trade, but, as unfortunately happens so often, they had no knowledge at all of how to keep their books.

They had now been trading for a year, and the taxman would soon be needing figures about their income. Tom came to their rescue. He was delighted to help because here was a new challenge. Where would he start, since the records were so incomplete?

Mandy and Penny were able to supply the following information. The business started on January 1, 1985. They had £1,000 cash in the till. The till was second-hand and cost £150. They had bought new shelves and display units for £2,500. The stock at the start, valued at £2,300, was bought on credit from Bella Donna Products Limited. A second-hand van, purchased from a friend, cost £1,350.

When Tom sorted out the numerous receipts and invoices for the year he discovered the following:

- the receipts from the till totalled £18,730
- the creditors had been paid a total of £10,073
- various expenses, such as heating and lighting, wrapping paper, cleaning, telephone, etc., totalled £570
- the rent and rates for the year was £1,640, of which £40 rent was paid in advance
- the money still to be received from the debtors at December 31 was £1,000 (this was the amount that the credit card company would reimburse Mandy and Penny for the goods they had sold on credit to the credit company's clients)
- money due to Mandy and Penny's creditors amounted to £2,100
- their notebook showed drawings of £960
- at December 31 Mandy checked the items of stock unsold and valued them at £2,210
- Tom decided that the van should be depreciated by £250 in the accounts

We will show the various stages Tom followed in order to prepare Mandy's and Penny's final accounts from these **incomplete records**.

The statement of affairs

The assets and liabilities at the start of the business must be listed in order to arrive at the capital or net worth.

To do this a statement called a **statement of affairs** is prepared. This is similar to an opening journal entry or balance sheet, but whereas the entries recorded in the journal and balance sheet are always taken from proven figures, those shown in a statement of affairs are based on estimated or incomplete records.

For example, in Mandy's and Penny's case the cash record is just a list of the receipts and payments for the year. Again, there is no total for the sales and purchases, just a record of the cash transactions for these items.

Here is the statement of affairs which Tom prepared for Mandy's and Penny's business, showing their capital at January 1, 1985.

Statement of affairs

MANDY & PENNY TIPTREE

STATEMENT OF AFFAIRS

As at January 1, 1985

	£	£
Stock	2,300	
Cash in till	1,000	
Till	150	
Shelves, display units	2,500	
Van	1,350	
Creditor:		
Bella Donna Products Ltd		2,300
Capital (net worth)		5,000
	£7,300	£7,300

The cash account

The cash transactions were then entered in a **cash account**, the figures being taken from the till receipts and the creditors receipted bills.

Cash account

MANDY & PENNY TIPTREE										
DR				**CASH ACCOUNT**						**CR**
Date	Details	Folio	£	p	Date	Details	Folio	£	p	
	RECEIPTS					PAYMENTS				
1985					1985					
Jan. 1	Balance		1,000		Dec. 31	Creditors for the				
Dec. 31	Till receipts		18,730			year		10,073		
					Dec. 31	Various expenses		570		
					Dec. 31	Rent/rates		1,640		
					Dec. 31	Drawings		960		
					Dec. 31	Balance	c/d	6,487		
			£19,730					£19,730		
1986										
Jan. 1	Balance	b/d	£6,487							

The final accounts (including VAT)

To prepare the trading account Tom had to find:

- the total sales for the year
- the total purchases for the year, net of 15% input VAT.

At this point Tom found some calculations were necessary. They are shown below.

1) To find the total sales for the year:

	£
Cash receipts from the till	18,730
Add The balance due from the credit card company at December 31	1,000
Total sales for the year	£19,730*

*Not subject to output VAT because the threshold has not been reached

2) To find the total purchases for the year:

	£
Cash paid to creditors	10,073
Less Amount outstanding at the start (Bella Donna Products Limited)	2,300
	£7,773
Add Creditors awaiting payment at December 31	2,100
Purchases for the year (inclusive of VAT)	£9,873
Less 15% input VAT	£1,288*
Total purchases for the year	£8,585 (net of VAT)†

Having the totals for the sales and purchases Tom was then able to prepare the input VAT account, the trading account, the profit and loss account and the balance sheet.

The input VAT account

INPUT VAT ACCOUNT V1									
DR									**CR**
Date	Details	Folio	£	p	Date	Details	Folio	£	p
1985									
Dec 31	Purchases	PA1	1,288	—					

*The figure to be used for the VAT and profit and loss accounts
† The figure to be used for the trading account

The trading account

Trading account

MANDY & PENNY TIPTREE

TRADING ACCOUNT

Year ended December 31, 1985

	£		£
Stock at start	2,300	Sales	19,370
Purchases	8,585		
	10,885		
Less Stock at December 31, 1985	2,210		
	8,675		
Balance being gross profit c/d to profit and loss a/c	11,055		
	£19,730		£19,730

The profit and loss account

Profit and loss account

MANDY & PENNY TIPTREE

PROFIT AND LOSS ACCOUNT

Year ended December 31, 1985

	£	£		£
Various expenses		570	Gross profit b/d from trading acount	11,055
Rent and rates	1,640			
Less Rent in advance	40	1,600		
Input VAT		1,288		
Depreciation				
Van		250		
Balance being net profit for the year		7,347		
		£11,055		£11,055

207

The balance sheet

Balance sheet

MANDY & PENNY TIPTREE
BALANCE SHEET
As at December 31, 1985

LIABILITIES	£	£	ASSETS	£	£
Capital	5,000		Fixed assets		
Add Net profit	7,347		Till		150
			Shelves & display		
	12,347		units		2,500
Less Drawings	960	11,387	Van	1,350	
			Less Depreciation	250	
					1,100
					3,750
Current Liabilities					
Creditor:		2,100			
Bella Donna Products					
			Current assets		
			Stock unsold	2,210	
			Debtor:		
			credit card co.	1,000	
			Cash at bank	6,000	
			Cash in till	487	
			Rent in advance	40	
					9,737
		£13,487			£13,487

Further aspects

The cash account for the trading period

In Mandy's and Penny's business all the transactions during the year were made by cash. At the end of the year, Tom transferred £6,000 into a bank account for them.

In other businesses the following items would also be taken into account when preparing a cash account from incomplete records.

1)   If the trader has a bank account then payments made and money received can be checked from the bank statement. The balance of the bank monies can therefore be proven.

2)   The figure for cash received can be obtained from the till receipts. Any extra money which the business has received should also be included. For example, the owner could win a sum of money on the football pools and pay it into the business. (There may be only verbal proof in such cases.)

Extra money such as pools winnings must be treated as *capital* and shown in the balance sheet. It is received from a source *other* than the business.

For example, suppose during the year Mandy invested winnings of £1,000, the balance sheet entry would then be:

	£
Capital at start	5,000
Add New investment	1,000
	£6,000

3)   It is quite a common custom for the owner to pay expenses from the till and omit to record it. This will also have to be taken into account when arriving at a cash balance.

Calculations for the sales and purchases totals for the year

When answering examination questions a number of calculations may be required.

Here is a method of presenting neatly the sales and purchases figures for the year. (We will again use Mandy's and Penny's figures for the example.)

To find:

	Sales £		*Purchases* £
Cash received from debtors for the year	18,730	Cash paid to creditors for the year	10,073
Less Debtors at the start of the year	—	*Less* Creditors at the start of the year	2,300
	£18,730		£7,773
Add Debtors at the end of the year	1,000	*Add* Creditors at the end of the year	2,100
Answer: Sales for the year	£19,730	*Answer:* Purchases for the year	£9,873

VAT accounts are to be prepared if required by the examiners.

Worked example

Kevin and Mary Foster have a small dairy farm. They are so busy working on the farm that they have no time to keep proper books of accounts.

They require: a set of final accounts for the milking section to be prepared for the year ended December 31, 1985.

For the purpose of this exercise VAT will be ignored.

They have supplied the following information:

1) All their cash receipts and payments are made through their bank. A summary of their bank account shows:

Receipts	£	Payments	£
Balance at Jan 1, 1985,	1000	Salaries	2,200
Marketing Board	19,080	Wages	1,050
Debtors	7,170	New milking machine	205
		Various expenses	650
		Drawings	1,000
		Creditors	15,300

2) During the year their family was supplied with milk to the value of £200.

3) The following information is also available:

	As at Jan. 1, 1985 £	As at Dec. 31, 1985 £
Stock (cattle food)	3,140	4,206
Debtors: Marketing Board	2,000	5,700
Others	950	1,000
Milking parlour	8,660	8,660
Equipment	840	961
Creditors	1,370	2,070

4) You are to depreciate the equipment valued at £840 by 10%.

Solution

Statement of affairs

KEVIN & MARY FOSTER

STATEMENT OF AFFAIRS

As at January 1, 1985

	£	£	£
Stock at Jan. 1, 1985		3,140	
Debtors:			
Marketing Board	2,000		
Others	950	2,950	
Creditors (various)			1,370
Milking parlour		8,660	
Equipment		840	
Bank		1,000	
Capital			15,220
		£16,590	£16,590

Cash account

KEVIN & MARY FOSTER									
DR			**CASH ACCOUNT**						**CR**
Date	Details	Folio	£	p	Date	Details	Folio	£	p
Jan. 1	Bank		1,000		Dec. 31	Salaries		2,200	
Dec. 31	Marketing Board		19,080		Dec. 31	Wages		1,050	
Dec. 31	Debtors		7,170		Dec. 31	New equipment		205	
					Dec. 31	Expenses		650	
					Dec. 31	Drawings		1,000	
					Dec. 31	Creditors		15,300	
					Dec. 31	Balance c/d		6,845	
			£27,250					£27,250	
Jan. 1	Balance b/d		£6,845						

Calculations to find:

		Sales			Purchases
	£	£			£
Cash received for the year:			Payments for the year:		15,300
Marketing Board	19,080				
Debtors	7,170	26,250	Less Creditors at Jan. 1, 1985		1,370
Less Debtors at Jan. 1, 1985		2,950			
		23,300			13,930
Add Debtors at Dec. 31, 1985			Add Creditors at Dec. 31, 1985		2,070
Marketing Board	5,700				
Others	1,000	6,700			
		£30,000			£16,000

Trading account

KEVIN & MARY FOSTER
TRADING ACCOUNT (MILKING SECTION)
Year ended December 31, 1985

	£	£		£
Stock (cattle food) at Jan. 1, 1985		3,140	Sales	30,000
Purchases	16,000			
Less Drawings in kind	200			
		15,800		
		18,940		
Wages		1,050		
		19,990		
Less Stock in hand Dec. 31, 1985		4,206		
Cost of milk sales		15,784		
Balance being gross profit c/d to profit and loss account		14,216		
		£30,000		£30,000

Profit and loss account

KEVIN & MARY FOSTER
PROFIT AND LOSS ACCOUNT (MILKING SECTION)
Year ended December 31, 1985

	£		£
Salaries	2,200	Gross profit b/d from trading a/c	14,216
Various expenses	650		
Depreciation:			
Equipment 10% × £840	84		
Balance being net profit for the year	11,282		14,216
	£14,216		£14,216

Balance sheet

KEVIN & MARY FOSTER

BALANCE SHEET

As at December 31, 1985

LIABILITIES	£	£	£	ASSETS	£	£
Capital		15,220		Fixed assets		
Add Net profit		11,282		Milking parlour		8,660
		26,502		Equipment	840	
				Less Depreciation	84	
Less Drawings						756
Cash	1,000			New equipment		205
In kind	200					9,621
		1,200	25,302			
				Current assets		
Current liabilities				Stock	4,206	
Creditors			2,070	Debtors	6,700	
				Cash at bank	6,845	
						17,751
			£27,372			£27,372

214

Chapter 16 Exercises

Preparation of final accounts from incomplete records

1 On July 1, 1985, D. Georgiou, a baker and confectioner, had the following assets and liabilities:

Cash in hand	£860
Cash at bank	£2,000
Stock	£5,600
Debtors	£13,821
Creditors	£8,900
Premises	£12,000
Vans	£3,400
Furniture and fittings	£2,000

He did not keep proper records of his business transactions but his diary of cash received and paid showed the following figures for the year:

Receipts:

Cash received for sales	£26,100

Payments:

Cash paid to creditors	£18,000
Various expenses	£825
Rent and rates paid	£1,500
Drawings (12 × £300 per month)	£3,600 for the year
New furniture	£276

At the end of the year, June 30, 1986, he had:

Stock unsold valued	£1,850
Creditors	£5,424
Debtors	£9,650

The furniture, value £2,000, is to be depreciated by 10%

The vans, value £3,400, are to be depreciated by 10%.

Rent paid includes £80 paid in advance.

You are to prepare for D. Georgiou a trading account and a profit and loss account for the year ended June 30, 1986, together with a balance sheet as at that date. VAT accounts are not required.

(N.B. : All calculations must be shown.)

2 *Alma Rushton, trading as the Top Fashion Dress Shop, did not keep proper books of account. You are asked to prepare a VAT account (for the sales and purchases only) and the final accounts from the following information at the year ended August 31, 1985.*

The assets and liabilities at the start of the year (September 1, 1984) were:

Cash at bank	£14,140
Cash in hand	£1,525
Sundry debtors (credit card company)	£12,275
Stock	£5,100
Display units	£3,900
Furniture	£5,300
Sundry creditors	£9,222

The summary of the cash book for the year ended August 31, 1985, was:

Receipts	£	Payments	£
Till receipts for cash sales	16,934	Creditors	17,155
Debtors (credit card customers)	10,752	Drawings	8,050
		Rent/rates	1,450
		Lighting/heating	1,025
		Decoration of showroom	2,950
		Wages	1,550
		Decoration of premises	1,960
		New carpet for showroom	1,000

You also have the following information:

- *the stock unsold at August 31 was valued at £4,850*
- *there were debtors of £10,725 and creditors of £11,238*
- *Alma took stock valued at £234 for her own use*
- *the rates paid in advance were £150*
- *VAT at 15%.*

(N.B.: Show clearly all your calculations.)

3 *Brian Parker, a jeweller, was made redundant by his employers and he invested his redundancy money in starting his own business on May 1, 1985.*

He rented a shop in the High Street and utilising the existing shopfittings he only needed to buy one extra display unit. This cost £2,900. He bought stock valued at £10,290, and put £14,000 into his bank account.

The only records of his business transactions for the year ended April 30, 1986, were contained in notebook form. The summary of his bank account was:

Receipts	£	Payments	£
Balance at May 1, 1985	14,000	Drawings	10,500
New investments (winnings		Creditors	28,818
from competition)	1,000		
		Various expenses	4,620
Receipts from sales	45,500		
		New safe	2,500
		Burglar alarm system	
		(Intruder)	1,000
		Showroom carpets	2,650

At April 30, 1986 (the year end), the outstanding invoices were:

Rent due	£300
Advertising (press)	£483
Insurance premiums	£500
Decorating	£2,000
Stock in hand	£15,000

During the year Brian took stock valued at £200 for presents. He had debtors £8,500 and creditors £12,400.

Prepare a VAT account for the sales and purchases only, a trading and a profit and loss account for the year ended April 30, 1986, and a balance sheet as at that date.

Answers are given in the *Worked Solutions.*

17

Limited Companies I

The growth of a business

As Tom and his business partner W. Wainwright saw their business progressing satisfactorily they decided to seek advice from their bank manager about possible future development. The bank manager naturally congratulated Tom on his good work but suggested that it would be prudent to make sure the partnership remained steady for the time being. However, it would be a good idea for Tom to consider what might be possible in a few years' time. He then outlined the gradual process of a business growing from that of a sole trader into a partnership and then to becoming a private limited company.

The sole trader

We know that at the start of his business Tom was a sole trader. He provided all the capital and was responsible for all the liabilities. The advantage of such a business was that Tom was his own boss, he could do whatever he wished within the limits of his trade. He did not need a legal agreement before commencing his business. The major disadvantage was that in the event of the failure of the business he would be entirely responsible for monies owed to his creditors. He could lose all his personal possessions (house, car, etc.), there being no limit to what could be used to cover his debts.

The partnership

The partnership with W. Wainwright was governed by a legally binding agreement, the partnership deed. The advantages were to increase the capital, and have the responsibility of the business shared with another. This meant that the liability for the debts would also be shared according to the terms of the partnership deed. There was still, however, the danger that in the event of the failure of the business the private possessions of both partners could be used to meet the debts owing to the creditors. Fortunately Tom's partnership business seemed to be flourishing so he and his partner were entitled to be ambitious.

The limited company

The next stage would be to consider forming a **limited company**. The advantage for Tom and his partner would be that in a limited company shares are bought to provide the capital, and liability is limited to the amount owing from the face value of the shares which have been bought at the time when the company ceases to trade. Those who buy shares are called **shareholders** and are the 'members', that is the owners, of the company.

Private and public limited companies

There are two types of limited company – a **private** limited company and a **public** limited company. The difference between the private company and the public company is not so much the size of the company but the fact that the private limited company restricts the sale of its shares to private members.

A *private* limited company can have a minimum of two members and there is no maximum number. The same rule applies to a *public* limited company but the Companies Act 1985 states that it must have at least £50,000 capital before it can go public.

So Tom and his partner could become a private limited company themselves, two members being sufficient. This would not, however, give them any advantage over their existing partnership since they would need extra capital for the expansion of the business, and this can only come from new members (shareholders).

Forming a limited company

The next step for them when the time is right would be to offer family and friends the opportunity to invest in their business by buying shares. Each member, the shareholder, would purchase a number of shares of, say, £1 each and form the private limited company of Robinson & Wainwright Limited.

It is important to note here that the partners would offer the purchase of the shares to 'family and friends'. This is because a private company is restricted to selling shares to private members. A public limited company advertises the shares in the press and issues a prospectus inviting the public to buy shares. A public limited company must have the initials 'PLC' after its name.

Whether the firm is a private or a public limited company it is governed by the companies' legislation of 1948 to 1981, consolidated into the single Companies Act 1985. This Act gives protection to the shareholders as well as to the creditors.

At the start of the proposed company a number of important documents must be completed and sent to the office of the Registrar of Companies in London to be filed. These documents are:

- **Memorandum of Association** which contains details of the name and address of the company's registered office, the objects and scope of the company and its method of finance (this is later called its authorised capital – see page 221);
- **Articles of Association** which contain the method of appointment of the directors, the voting rights of the shareholders and the division of the dividends.

If these documents are approved, the Registrar issues a **certificate of incorporation** which is the authority for the new company to commence trading as a limited company. (In the case of a public limited company a **trading certificate** is also issued.)

Classes of shares

There are many different types of share in a company, each having particular advantages and disadvantages. The most common types of share are described below.

Ordinary shares

These are shares which do not carry a fixed percentage of profit called a **dividend**. They are also known as risk shares, and ordinary shareholders are in effect risk-bearers of the company.

If the profits are good in one year, an ordinary shareholder with, say, 500 ordinary shares of £1 each might receive 20% of the holding as a dividend, that is £100 (less tax). If in the next year the firm did not make sufficient profit to award a dividend, then this shareholder would not receive any dividend, hence the risk.

Preference shares

These are shares which, as the name implies, have preference over the ordinary shares when the company's profits are being divided.

Preference shares carry a fixed percentage of dividend payable every year. For example, if a shareholder has 1,000 7% preference shares of £1 each, he or she will receive an annual dividend of £70 (less tax), if there is sufficient profit to be shared.

Preference shares are subdivided into two categories:

- non-cumulative preference shares;
- cumulative preference shares.

Non-cumulative preference shares

These are shares which are only payable out of the profits for the *particular year*. If the company does not make sufficient profit then a dividend is not paid for that year.

Cumulative preference shares

These shares guarantee that even if a dividend is not paid in one year then the arrears accumulate and must be added to the dividend for the next year or are carried forward until a payment can be made.

Capital of limited companies

All the shares described in the previous section form the capital of a company but further explanation is necessary before we can begin to prepare the company accounts.

Authorised capital

This is the maximum number of shares which the company can offer for sale to prospective shareholders (whether ordinary or preference). It is the number shown in the memorandum of association and is also known as the **nominal** or **registered capital**.

Issued capital

This is the amount of capital actually *issued* for sale to the public. It is usually only part of the authorised capital as the company only 'calls up' sufficient for immediate needs. It is also called **subscribed capital**.

Called-up capital

This is the amount due to the company. Not all of it will have been received. For example, a shareholder may contract to buy 100 £1 ordinary shares. The company may require an immediate payment (first call) of £25. The second call of £50 may be made one month later. The balance, £25, is classed as a 'call in arrear', and represents the limit of the shareholders' indebtedness to the company in the event of the company ceasing to trade (if it is **wound up**).

Some shareholders prefer to pay their shares in advance (before the company 'calls' them). These are classed as 'calls in advance'.

Paid-up capital

This is the amount that has been paid by the shareholders for their shares.

Debenture or loan stock

When a company needs to borrow money for a long term in order to extend its business it is customary for it to do so by issuing **debentures**. These are loans for which the company is in debt to the lenders who are called **debenture loaders**. The loans are repayable in full plus a fixed charge for the interest.

Debenture holders are *not* shareholders. The interest due to them *must* be paid whether the company makes a profit or a loss. Debenture interest is an *expense* and must be debited to the profit and loss account.

For example, T. Ho & Company Limited issued 100 10% debenture shares at £200 each. This means the company borrowed £20,000 as capital. Every year £2,000 interest must be paid (generally paid half-yearly). This will continue over a fixed period of years and then the £20,000 capital must be repaid.

Fixed charge debentures

These are loans the security for which is charged against a specified fixed asset of the company. If the interest is not paid regularly the debenture holders are said to have a 'claim against the fixed asset' – they have a right to sell the asset in order to obtain the loan repayment in the event of the company being wound up. The debenture holders will be paid out of the proceeds of the sale of the specific asset to which their debenture applies.

Floating charge debentures

These are loans the security for which is charged against the circulating (current) assets of the company. It is customary for this to relate specifically to the stock.

The business entity

It is important to remember that in every business there is a distinction between the owners and the firm itself. The owners have a claim on the firm which 'owes' them an income from the money that has been invested in it. Equally the firm has a life of its own and so it is not liable for any private expenses of the owners.

This difference whereby the firm is considered to have a separate identity gives rise to the concept of the **business entity**.

The main differences between ownership and management are:

- *The sole trader.* He or she *owns and manages* the business, *providing* the capital and taking the profits, and has unlimited liability for the debts.
- *The partnership.* Capital is *provided* by the partners who own and often manage the business and share the profits and losses according to the partnership deed. If a partnership deed has not been drawn up at the time the firm ceases to trade, the Partnership Act of 1890 applies. All the partners have unlimited liability for the debts.
- *Limited companies.* The shareholders *provide* the *capital* and are the *owners* of the business. The company is *managed* by a board of directors appointed by the shareholders. These directors are paid a salary and business expenses, both of which are charged to the profit and loss account. Limited Companies are controlled by the Companies Act 1985 and must trade within the limits of the company's memorandum and articles of association (see page 219).

Final accounts of a limited company

Limited companies prepare their final accounts in the same order as other businesses – the manufacturing account (where applicable), the trading account, the profit and loss account and a balance sheet. Differences arise, however, in the second half of the profit and loss account, that is, in the appropriation account, which must be carried through to the balance sheet.

1) The debit side of the appropriation account

The allocation of the profits is:

- goodwill and the depreciation of goodwill;
- reserves – revenue reserve, general reserve and capital reserve;
- the dividends proposed for each class of share;
- the balance (undistributed profit).

Goodwill

Goodwill is the price the owner of an established business or profession adds to the assets when he or she is selling the business as a going concern. It is, as it were, a price charged for the hard work the owner has done to create a good business reputation for his or her personality, the product sold, or even the favourable location of the premises.

In book-keeping it is called an *intangible asset* because, unlike the other assets, it cannot be seen to be real.

When the selling price of a retail business is agreed between the purchaser and the seller the price paid for the goodwill is usually based on turnover.

In other businesses the price for goodwill is based on the average net profits for a period of years – one to five years in the following simple example:

		£
Year 1	Net profit	2,500
Year 2	Net profit	6,000
Year 3	Net profit	8,000
Year 4	Net profit	8,000
Year 5	Net profit	7,000
	Total	£31,500

The average profit for one year will be:

£31,500 ÷ 5 = £6,300 per year.

The purchaser could estimate that it might take three years to build up the profits and the goodwill of the former owner. Therefore he/she might consider £18,900 to be a fair price to pay for that goodwill.

223

Depreciation of goodwill

Businesses frequently write off goodwill by means of depreciation. It cannot, however, be written off in the profit and loss account because, being an intangible asset, it is not a revenue loss. It is therefore written off as a loss in the appropriation account, and shown in the balance sheet as an intangible asset.

Extract of BALANCE SHEET as at December 31, 1985			
Assets			
Intangible asset	Cost	Depreciation	Net
Goodwill			
Balance at Jan. 1, 1985	£500	£500	—
	—		—

Revenue reserve

These are amounts which the directors consider should be retained by the company, for example for the replacement or purchase of a new fixed asset.

General reserve

This is an amount to be retained for any purpose the directors decide. It may be retained to compensate for a year when perhaps a below average profit has resulted. The company will be able to keep the shareholders from losing confidence in their company by subsidising the dividends paid to the ordinary shareholders.

Capital reserve

This is the amount of capital which the directors retain and which will not be used for payment of dividends. It is made up of:

- the increase in value of certain fixed assets such as land and buildings;
- profits prior to incorporation, that is the profits which were made before the company became public.

The difference between a provision and a reserve.

- A **provision** was described in Chapter 6 (page 82) as a *charge* set aside from the profits for an *anticipated* expense – bad debts. It is to 'provide' for something that may happen in the future.

  A provision is always debited to the *profit and loss account.*

- A **reserve** is an appropriation of the profit which is not a *charge* but represents *the amount the directors have decided* should be retained for the benefit of the company.

  A reserve is always debited to the *appropriation account.*

Dividends and balance

The position of these items on the debit side of the appropriation account is shown below.

2) The credit side of the appropriation account

- The balance of the appropriation account (undistributed profit) is brought down from the previous year.
- The net profit is brought down from the profit and loss account for the current year.

3) The appropriation account

As an example we will now prepare an appropriation account from the following information supplied by the Timber-Wolf Logging Company Limited:

1985		
Jan. 1	Balance of the appropriation account b/d	£32,700
Dec. 31	Profit for the year (after tax)	£18,500
	Transfer to reserve for machinery	£9,000
	Transfer to general reserve	£9,000
	Proposed dividend on 5% preference shares	£2,000
	Proposed dividend on 5% ordinary shares	£7,000
	Goodwill to be written off	£200

THE TIMBER-WOLF LOGGING COMPANY LIMITED
APPROPRIATION ACCOUNT
year ended December 31, 1985

1985		£	1985		£
Dec. 31	Goodwill (written off)	200	Jan. 1	Balance b/d	32,700
	Reserve		1985		
	Machinery	9,000	Dec. 31	Net profit for the year	18,500
	General reserve	9,000			
	Dividends				
	5% Preference shares	2,000			
	5% Ordinary shares	7,000			
	Balance (being undistributed profit)	24,000			
		£51,200			£51,200

The appropriation account given in the traditional horizontal format above may also be presented in vertical format:

THE TIMBER-WOLF LOGGING COMPANY LIMITED
APPROPRIATION ACCOUNT
year ended December 31, 1985

		£	£
1985			
Jan. 1	Balance b/d		32,700
Dec. 31	Net profit for the year		18,500
			£51,200
Dec. 31	Goodwill (written off)	200	
	Reserves - machinery	9,000	
	General	9,000	
		18,200	
	Proposed dividends		
	5% Preference shares	2,000	
	5% Ordinary shares	7,000	
		27,200	
	Balance (being undistributed profit) c/d to the balance sheet	24,000	
			£51,200

Exercises on limited companies are to be found on pages 236–40, at the end of the following chapter which covers further aspects of the same subject.

18

Limited Companies II

The balance sheet

The Companies Act 1985 requires the balance sheet of a limited company to contain more information than the balance sheet of a sole trader or a partnership. This is to safeguard the interests of the shareholders.

A sole trader or a partner is usually involved in the conducting of the business and therefore should have knowledge of the financial state of the business. Shareholders, on the other hand, are rarely involved in the actual running of the firm and therefore they need all the information necessary for them to understand the financial affairs of their company.

In practice the preparation a company balance sheet is done by the company secretary and/or the company accountant. As it is specialised work, they have considerable knowledge of company legislation which includes taxation, investments, etc., and these are beyond the scope of this book.

We will now prepare a limited company balance sheet showing only the basic requirements of the Companies Act.

The order of the groups of assets and liabilities is similar to that of the balance sheet of a sole trader, but particular emphasis must be given in the presentation of the *assets* and the *capital* which is invested by the shareholders who are the owners of the company.

Assets

Fixed assets

Plant, machinery, vehicles and fixtures and fittings, etc., must be recorded so as to show:

- the initial cost;
- the aggregate (that is the total) depreciation;
- the net value (the written down value).

Current assets

These are grouped in the same way as for the balance sheet of a sole trader and partnership (see Chapters 4 and 11). In addition, the preference share dividend which has been paid during the year and interim ordinary share dividends are listed as current assets.

Current liabilities

These are grouped in the same way as for the balance sheet of a sole trader and partnership (see Chapters 4 and 11). There is an added entry for the proposed dividends which have not yet been paid to the shareholders.

Working capital

This is the balance from the current assets after deducting the current liabilities (see Chapter 8).

Fictitious assets

These are the preliminary expenses – legal charges, registration fees, etc., which are necessary before the limited company can commence trading. These are considered as 'assets' because they were part of the foundation of the company.

Long-term liabilities

Bank loans, mortgages and amounts due to hire purchase companies are recorded here in the same way as in the balance sheet of the sole trader and partnership. These are shown as in the balance sheet on page 108.

If the company has issued debenture shares the total amount of the loan must be entered as a long-term liability. There should be a note as to which asset of the company has been given as a security for the loan.

Liabilities

These are entered immediately below the assets on the balance sheet in the following order:

    a)   the authorised capital (as defined on page 221);
    b)   the issued or subscribed capital (as defined on page 221);

> - 'Calls in arrears' are deducted   } see page 221.
> - 'Calls in advance' are added

    c)   reserves:

- the opening balance of the reserve account to which is added:
- the new reserve transferred from the appropriation account;
- the balance of the appropriation account (that is the undistributed profit).

The final accounts

Following all the previous instructions we will now prepare a limited company's final accounts.

Trial balance of Timber-Wolf Logging Company Limited

THE TIMBER-WOLF LOGGING COMPANY LIMITED
TRIAL BALANCE
year ended December 31, 1985

	Debit Balances £	Credit Balances £
Cash at bank	16,000	
Forestry land	110,000	
Machinery & tools	20,000	
Lorries and vehicles	35,000	
Office furniture and fittings	12,000	
Stock of timber at Jan. 1, 1985	17,148	
Debtors	30,000	
Sales (timber)		70,848
Creditors		12,000
Purchases (soil dressings etc.)	20,000	
Wages	12,500	
Salaries	10,000	
Office expenses	2,500	
Repairs	2,000	
5% preference shares at £1 each (fully paid)		40,000
Ordinary shares at £1 each (75p called up)		105,000
Reserve balance at Jan. 1, 1985		32,700
Preliminary expenses	2,000	
Goodwill	200	
6% debenture shares		30,000
Debenture interest (½ year)	1,200	
	£290,548	£290,548

The trial balance on the previous page was taken from the books of the Timber-Wolf Logging Company Limited on December 31, 1985. You are to prepare:

- the trading account;
- the profit and loss account;
- the company's appropriation account;
- the balance sheet (in vertical style) as at December 31, 1985.

The following information must also be taken into account:

- the authorised share capital is made up of:
  40,000   5% preference shares of £1 each;
  140,000   ordinary shares of £1 each;
- stock of timber at December 31, 1985 was £26,000;
- depreciation to be accounted for as follows:

Machinery and tools	£5,000
Vehicles	£7,500
Furniture and fittings	£500

- goodwill of £200 is to be written off;
- the directors have decided to pay 5% dividend on the ordinary shares, and to transfer £9,000 to the reserve machinery account, and £9,000 to the general reserve.

Trading account of Timber-Wolf Logging Company Limited

THE TIMBER-WOLF LOGGING COMPANY LIMITED
TRADING ACCOUNT
year ended December 31, 1985

	£		£
Stock at Jan. 1, 1985	17,148	Sales	70,848
Purchases	20,000		
	37,148		
Wages	12,500		
	49,648		
Less stock at Dec. 31, 1985	26,000		
Cost of goods sold	23,648		
Gross profit c/d to profit and loss account	47,200		
	£70,848		£70,848

Profit and loss account of Timber-Wolf Logging Company Limited

THE TIMBER-WOLF LOGGING COMPANY LIMITED PROFIT & LOSS ACCOUNT year ended December 31, 1985				
		£		£
Salaries		10,000	Gross profit b/d from trading account	47,200
Repairs		2,000		
Office expenses		2,500		
Debenture interest ½ year		1,200		
Depreciation				
Machinery	5,000			
Vehicles	7,500			
Furniture/fittings	500	13,000		
Net profit		18,500		
		£47,200		£47,200

Appropriation account of Timber-Wolf Logging Company Limited

THE TIMBER-WOLF LOGGING COMPANY LIMITED APPROPRIATION ACCOUNT, year ended December 31, 1985					
		£			£
1985			1985		
Dec. 31	Goodwill	200	Jan. 1	Balance b/d	32,700
	Reserve				
	Machinery	9,000	Dec. 31	Net profit b/d for the year	18,500
	General reserve	9,000			
	Dividends				
	5% preference shares	2,000			
	5% ordinary shares*	5,250			
	Balance	25,750			
		£51,200			£51,200

*5% of £105,000 'called up' ordinary share capital.

Balance sheet of Timber-Wolf Logging Company Limited (vertical format)

THE TIMBER-WOLF LOGGING COMPANY LIMITED
BALANCE SHEET
as at 31 December, 1985

ASSETS

	Cost	Depreciation	Net (Written down value)
Intangible asset	£	£	£
Goodwill (written off)	200	200	—
Fixed assets			
Forestry land	110,000		110,000
Machinery/tools	20,000	5,000	15,000
Lorries/vehicles	35,000	7,500	27,500
Office furniture/fittings	12,000	500	11,500
	177,200	13,200	£164,000

	£	£
Current assets		
Stock of timber	26,000	
Debtors	30,000	
Bank	16,000	72,000
Less		
Current liabilities		
Creditors	12,000	
Proposed dividends		
5% preference shares	2,000	
5% ordinary shares	5,250	19,250

continued on next page

Working capital			52,750
Fictitious asset –			
preliminary expenses			2,000
			218,750
Less long term liabilities			
6% debentures (secured on forestry land)			30,000
			£188,750

LIABILITIES	Authorised	Issued	
Share capital	£	£	
5% preference shares of £1 each (fully paid)	40,000	40,000	
Ordinary shares of £1 each (75p called up)	140,000	105,000	
	£180,000	£145,000	
	£		
Reserves			
Machinery account	9,000		
General	9,000		
Balance of appropriation account	25,750	43,750	
			188,750

Worked examination question

Here is an example of an examination type of question requiring the preparation of a limited company's appropriation account and balance sheet, *after* the trading account and profit and loss account have been prepared.

The following balances remained in the books of the Teddy Bear Children's Clothing Company Limited at the end of their trading year September 30, 1985:

	£
Capital	
150,000 ordinary shares at £1 each (fully paid)	150,000
Machinery and equipment (at cost)	112,200
Delivery vans (at cost)	16,500
Showroom fittings (at cost)	17,710
Sundry debtors	22,000
Sundry creditors	9,360
Cash at bank	31,020
General reserve	10,000
Stock	38,000
Profit and loss account	
Credit balance b/f September 1, 1984	10,000
Net profit for the year	34,460
Depreciation	
Machinery and equipment	18,700
Delivery vans	3,300
Showroom fittings	1,610

Notes:
1) The authorised capital of the company is 200,000 ordinary shares at £1 each.
2) The directors decided to transfer £8,000 to the general reserve.
3) The recommended dividend is 15% on the ordinary shares.
4) The balance sheet must show:

- the totals of the fixed and current assets;
- the current liabilities;
- the total revenue reserves;
- the working capital;
- the written down (net) value of the fixed assets.

Solution

THE TEDDY BEAR CHILDREN'S CLOTHING COMPANY LIMITED
APPROPRIATION ACCOUNT, year ended September 30, 1985

1985		£	1985		£
Sept. 30	General reserve	8,000	Sept. 1	Balance b/d	10,000
✓	Dividend 15% ordinary shares	22,500	Sept. 30	Net profit for the year	34,460
✓	Balance being undistributed profit c/fwd	13,960			
		£44,460			£44,460

THE TEDDY BEAR CHILDREN'S CLOTHING COMPANY LIMITED
BALANCE SHEET, as at September 30, 1985

ASSETS	Cost	Depreciation	Net
Fixed assets	£	£	£
Machinery/equipment	112,200	18,700	93,500
Delivery Vans	16,500	3,300	13,200
Showroom Fittings	17,710	1,610	16,100
	146,410	23,610	122,800
Current assets	£	£	
Stock	38,000		
Debtors	22,000		
Bank	31,020	91,020	
Less			
Current liabilities			
Creditors	9,360		
Dividend 15% Ordinary Shares	22,500	31,860	
Working capital			59,160
			£181,960

LIABILITIES	Authorised	Issued	
Share capital	£	£	
Ordinary shares at £1 each	200,000	150,000	
Reserve	£		
General	10,000		
Add New	8,000	18,000	
Balance of appropriation Account		13,960	
			£181,960

Chapter 18 Exercises

1 *Panorama Photographs Ltd. had the balances given below in their books after the trading and profit and loss accounts had been prepared at March 31, 1986.*

You are to prepare the company's appropriation account and the balance sheet, noting the following decisions of the directors:

- *a dividend of 6% is to be paid for the preference shares;*
- *a dividend of 7% is recommended for the ordinary shares;*
- *the general reserve is to be increased by £3,000;*
- *depreciation is to be provided as follows;*

Furniture and fittings	*£870*
Equipment	*£2,200*
Cars	*£520*

- *a provision for bad debts is to be created at 5% of the debtors.*

	£
Share capital:	
20,000 6% preference shares at £1 each fully paid up	20,000
100,000 ordinary shares at £1 each – 60,000 called up	60,000
10,000 6% debentures at £1 each	10,000
Furniture and showroom fittings (at cost)	8,700
Premises	20,000
Equipment	22,000
Cars	5,200
Stock	30,200
Debtors	17,400
Creditors	6,485
General reserve	16,000
Balance of appropriation account at April 1, 1985	1,890
Net profit for the year	13,165
Preliminary expenses	2,000

2 *The Westoakhill Company Ltd. has an authorised capital of 200,000 £1 ordinary shares, 150,000 issued and fully paid up. There is also loan capital of 4,000 6% £5 debentures, £20,000.*

The following balances were extracted from the books on April 30, 1986:

Premises	£69,000
Machinery	£128,869
Stock	£22,065
Debtors	£26,950
Bank	£37,040
Creditors	£9,500

General reserve	£36,000
Net profit for the year	£38,000
Balance of appropriation account (representing undistributed profit) at April 1, 1985	£4,650

The directors decided to transfer £15,000 to the general reserve. A recommended dividend of 15% was approved for the ordinary shares.

You are required to prepare the appropriation account and the company's balance sheet as at April 30, 1986, allowing for depreciation of the machinery at 20% on cost.

3 *The Meadway Haulage Company Ltd. had an authorised capital of 60,000 7% £1 preference shares, 240,000 £1 ordinary shares are all paid up, and 30,000 6% £1 debentures.*

THE MEADWAY HAULAGE COMPANY LTD TRIAL BALANCE *year ended December 31, 1985*		
	Debit balances	Credit balances
Stock at 1 Jan., 1985	4,650	
Purchases	26,009	
Returns outward		402
Wages	8,650	
Sales		83,479
Office expenses	2,702	
Insurances	4,375	
Road tax	1,445	
Land	100,000	
Garages	201,500	
Equipment	23,520	
Motors/lorries	45,000	
Debtors	61,500	
Bank	18,025	
Creditors		32,645
Preliminary expenses	3,000	
6% debenture ($\frac{1}{2}$ year) interest	900	
60,000 7% preference shares		60,000
240,000 ordinary shares		240,000
6% debenture shares		30,000
Appropriation account balance at Jan. 1, 1985		54,750
	501,276	501,276

Stock in hand at 31 December, 1985 £13,000

From the trial balance on the previous page, prepare:

- *the trading account and profit and loss account;*
- *the company's appropriation account;*
- *the balance sheet as at December 31, 1985.*

The following additional information must be included in the accounts:

- *insurance prepaid £875;*
- *road tax due but not paid £55;*
- *six months debenture interest is outstanding;*
- *allow depreciation:*
  Motors and lorries   £7,500
  Equipment   £2,520

The directors propose:
- a dividend of 4% on the ordinary shares and 7% on the preference shares;
- £20,000 is to be transferred to the general reserve.

4 *The Singh Drapery Company Ltd has the following balances in its books after the trading and profit and loss accounts have been prepared for the year ended December 31, 1985.*

Authorised capital
    25,000   7% preference shares at £1 each fully paid up.
   100,000   ordinary shares at £1 each, 75,000 fully paid up

Creditors	£15,000
Debtors	£26,000
Stock	£10,000
Fixtures and fittings	£24,000 (cost)
Vans	£20,000 (cost)
Premises	£55,000
Cash at bank	£39,450
General reserve	£25,000
Profit and loss account for 1985 (credit)	£20,400
Preference dividend paid	£1,750
Appropriation account balance brought forward at January 1, 1985 (credit)	£6,800

The directors recommend:

- a transfer of £5,000 to the general reserve;
- a dividend of 10% on the ordinary shares.

You are required to:

- prepare the profit and loss appropriation account for the year ended December 31, 1985;
- provide for depreciation:
  - Fixtures and fittings   £4,000
  - Vans   £5,000
- Prepare a balance sheet, in the vertical style, as at December 31, 1985.

5 *The Marlboro Crescent Hotel Supply Co. Ltd has an authorised capital of:*

- 50,000   6% £1 preference shares fully paid up;
- 200,000   £1 ordinary shares 150,000 issued;
- 60,000   6% £1 debenture shares fully paid up.

THE MARLBORO CRESCENT HOTEL SUPPLY CO. LTD.
TRIAL BALANCE
year ended December 31, 1985

	£	£
6% preference shares at £1 each fully paid		50,000
Ordinary shares 200,000 £1 each		150,000
6% debentures		60,000
Goodwill	2,000	
Premises	120,000	
Vehicles	55,000	
Machinery	33,000	
Furniture and fittings	22,000	
Stock	15,400	
Purchases	124,240	
Returns outward		650
Wages	4,000	
Bad debts	500	
Salaries	3,000	
Repairs and maintenance/machines	2,000	
Office expenses	3,765	
Directors fees	3,000	
Sales		165,105
Debtors	51,250	
Bank	32,500	
Creditors		7,500
Preliminary expenses	2,500	
Debentures $\frac{1}{2}$ yearly	1,800	
Balance appropriation account		42,700
	£475,955	£475,955

Stock in hand at December 31, 1985, £30,800

From the trial balance you are to prepare:

- *a trading account, profit and loss account and appropriation account;*
- *a balance sheet as at December 31, 1985.*

The following items must be included in the accounts:

- *Deprecation:*
Motor vehicles	£5,000
Machinery	£3,000
Furniture/fittings	£2,000
- *a provision for bad debts is to be created at 4% of the debtors;*
- *debenture interest outstanding at December 31, 1985 was £1,800;*
- *goodwill (£2,000) is to be written off.*

The directors propose:

- *a dividend of 6% on the preference shares;*
- *a dividend of 10% on the ordinary shares;*
- *£10,000 to be transferred to the general reserve;*
- *£10,000 to be transferred to the revenue reserve.*

Answers are given in the *Worked Solutions.*

Postscript

It is hoped that people in business will have been given the opportunity to understand what is involved in keeping accurate records and to appreciate the work done by an accountant.

Anyone who has mastered the principles contained in Volumes 1 and 2 of this text should now have sufficient enthusiasm to begin studies leading to recognised qualifications from the examining bodies, or to consider training for accountancy.

Glossary

This glossary gives a short explanation of some of the terms that are in **bold print** in the text.

Adjustments Items such as provisions and accruals to be taken into account at the end of a trading period when the final accounts are being prepared. This is in order to give an accurate picture of the business's affairs.

Assets
- *Fixed*: plant, machinery, vehicles etc., purchased for long-term use in the business.
- *Current*: stock, debtors, cash, bank, proposed dividends to be paid to shareholders.
- *Fictitious*: preliminary expenses, e.g. legal charges, registration fees prior to the formation of the company.
- *Intangible*: goodwill.

Authorised capital This is the maximum number of shares which the company is authorised to offer for sale. It is stated in the *memorandum of association*.

Average stock Formula: $\dfrac{\text{Stock at start} + \text{Closing stock}}{2}$

Business entity The concept whereby the firm is considered to have a life of its own and is not responsible for the private drawings etc. of the owner.

Called-up capital This is the amount of money due to the company from the shareholders.

Capital The difference between the *assets* and *liabilities* (see Chapter 10, Volume 1).

Capital employed The total amount of capital being used in the business at the date of the balance sheet.
Formula: Total value of the assets − The debtors.

Capital expenses Money invested in plant, machinery, etc., which are intended for use over a number of years, e.g. plant and machinery used in a manufacturing business.

Capital reserve This is the amount of capital which the directors retain and which will not be used for payment of dividends. It is made up of:
- the increase in value of certain fixed assets such as land and buildings;
- profits prior to incorporation – that is, the profits which were made before the company became public.

Control accounts (also known as *total accounts*) Accounts which contain the total figures of the debtors and creditors, sales and purchases taken from subsidiary books.

Current account The account in partnership accounts wherein is recorded the salaries, interest on capital drawings and the share of the profit (or losses).

Debentures These are shares issued by a company in order to raise money for a specific purpose. (The debenture holders are *not* shareholders.) Debentures are loans which are repayable in full plus a fixed charge.

Depreciation	• *Equal instalment method*: Depreciation in the book value of an asset by means of the same amount each year in order to write the asset down to zero, e.g. a motor car. • *Diminishing balance method*: Depreciation by reducing an asset's book value by an agreed precentage each year. Commonly used for plant and machinery, furniture, etc., which will be in use for a period of years. • *Revaluation method*: Applies to such items as livestock, tools, etc., which are valued by an expert.
Direct or variable costs	Costs which can fluctuate and can be applied to a particular section of the production, i.e. wages, raw materials, carriage, etc.
Factory overheads	The other title for *indirect* or *fixed costs*.
Goodwill	This is the value added on to the selling price of a business which a firm allows for the hard work done by the owner in building up a prosperous business. It is an intangible asset.
Indirect or fixed costs	Expenses which are associated with the overheads and are separate from production, i.e. rent, rates, repairs and depreciation of machinery, etc.
Issued capital	This is the number of shares actually issued for sale to the public. Usually it is only part of the *authorised capital*.
Limited companies	• A *private limited company* is one which is restricted to selling shares to private members. The minimum number of members is two, and there is no maximum number. It has the words 'Co. Ltd' after the name. • A *public limited company* is one which advertises its shares and invites the public to buy them. The minimum number of members is two, and it must have a capital of at least £50,000 before it can go public. It has the initials 'PLC' after the name.
Limited liability	This refers to the amount which the shareholders are liable to have to pay if the company should cease trading. It is limited to the amount that the shareholder still owes on any shares which are not yet called up.
Manufacturing account	An account prepared to show the cost of production of the manufacturing of raw materials into finished products.
Memorandum of association	Document showing all the information relevant to a limited company.
Paid-up capital	This is the amount that has actually been paid so far by the shareholders.
Payments in advance	Monies paid before the due date must be subtracted from the figures shown in the trial balance. They are entered in the trading account and/or the profit & loss account and must be shown in the balance sheet.
Payments in arrears	These are, for example, rent, monies due and outstanding when the final accounts are being prepared. They are added to the figure given in the trial balance and are shown in the trading account and/or the profit & loss account, and must be shown in the balance sheet as a liability.
Percentage of net profit on turnover	This is a percentage of net sales given by the formula: $\dfrac{\text{Net profit}}{\text{Turnover}} \times 100$
Prime cost	The total cost of raw materials, labour, and direct expenses such as carriage in of raw materials.
Rate of stock turnover	The number of times the stock has been sold (turned into cash), given by the formula:

$$\frac{\text{Total cost of goods sold}}{\text{Average stock}}$$

Reserves

- *Revenue reserve*: The amount which the directors consider should be retained by the company for a definite purpose.
- *General reserve*: The amount retained for any purpose which might arise in the future.

Revenue expenses

Shown in the profit & loss account, such items as rent, rates, salaries, etc., which occur within the current trading period.

Shares

- *Ordinary shares*. These do not carry a fixed dividend. If the firm does not make sufficient profit the ordinary shareholder does not receive any dividend.
- *Preference shares*. These earn a fixed percentage payable every year. There are two types:

  a) *non-cumulative preference shares* are payable only out of the profits for a particular year;

  b) *cumulative preference shares* mean that the dividend accumulates so that if it is not paid one year it runs on until it can be paid.

Value Added Tax (VAT)

A tax levied by HM Customs and Excise on persons with more than a certain amount of taxable turnover per year. The amount and the rate are subject to alteration in the annual Budget.

Work in progress

Products which are only partly completed when the manufacturing account is being prepared. Work in progress at the *start* of the period is added to the direct or indirect costs. Work in progress at the *end* of the period is subtracted from the total of prime costs plus factory overheads.

Working capital ratio

Formula: Current assets − current liabilities

Index